What People Are Saying About

Revealing Light

Most of us could, if pressed, peel back the layers of the past and revisit the struggles that made us who we are, but it takes rare honesty and a high level of awareness to process the lessons learned and use them to help others navigate their own path more easily. Maryann has done that with this unforgettable memoir. It is enlightening, uplifting, moving, and lovingly written, and I am changed because of it. At the very least, I will never take a single day of my life for granted again. And neither will you.

Cash Peters, author of *Why Your Life Matters*

Maryann's book skilfully delves into the challenges of battling cancer, providing a poignant account that resonates with empathy. Beyond her personal journey, Maryann's exceptional abilities as a psychic reader and astrologer shine through, adding a unique and captivating dimension to her story. Her successful YouTube channel becomes a platform not just for psychic insights but also a beacon of hope for those of us looking for solace in this difficult world we live in now, politically as well as spiritually. The combination of vulnerability, psychic prowess, and success makes Maryann's book a compelling and inspiring read.

Linda Grindel, psychic/medium, *Linda G the Comanche Psychic* (YouTube)

T0321323

This book is ideal for anyone confronted with a cancer diagnosis or supporting someone through treatment.

Dr Lena Rodriguez, *Tarot Down Under* (YouTube) & co-creator of the *One World Tarot* deck

Maryann has written a courageous and wise memoir about her fight to survive cancer. Even more profound are the revelations she shares about her faith and how her cancer diagnosis and treatment opened the way for a new positivity and connection to the spiritual and divine. Always an empath, Maryann's journey beyond "surviving" to "thriving" post-cancer, has been truly transformative as anyone who follows her Revealing Light YouTube channel will know. She shares her intimate knowledge of tarot, astrology and more in this generous and engaging treasure.

Jacquelene Pearson, publisher, *The Point* (news website), and author of *Mother's Song,* a poetry collection

Revealing Light

How Cancer Illuminated
My Divine Blueprint

Shadowscape: The Stevie Vegas Chronicles
ISBN: 0992460522
Dawn of the Shadowcasters
ISBN: 1782794565
Blood Visions
ISBN: 9781681461410

Revealing Light

How Cancer Illuminated
My Divine Blueprint

Maryann Weston

BOOKS

London, UK
Washington, DC, USA

CollectiveInk

First published by O-Books, 2025
O-Books is an imprint of Collective Ink Ltd.,
Unit 11, Shepperton House, 89 Shepperton Road, London, N1 3DF
office@collectiveinkbooks.com
www.collectiveinkbooks.com
www.o-books.com

For distributor details and how to order please visit the 'Ordering' section on our website.

Text copyright: Maryann Weston, 2023

ISBN: 978 1 80341 730 1
978 1 80341 738 7 (ebook)
Library of Congress Control Number: 2023950595

A CIP catalogue record for this book is available from the British Library.

Design: Lapiz Digital Services

UK: Printed and bound by CPI Group (UK) Ltd, Croydon, CR0 4YY
Printed in North America by CPI GPS partners

The authors of this book do not dispense medical advice or prescribe the use of any technique as a form of treatment for physical, emotional, or medical problems without the advice of a physician, either directly or indirectly. The intent of the authors is only to offer information of a general nature to help you in your quest for emotional and spiritual well-being. In the event you use any of the information in this book for yourself, which is your constitutional right, the authors and the publisher assume no responsibility for your actions.

We operate a distinctive and ethical publishing philosophy in all areas of our business, from our global network of authors to production and worldwide distribution.

Contents

I now understand that we go on beyond this life ... into the light of home, not the darkness of oblivion.

This book is dedicated to my beautiful sister Jane who had the same cancer as me, in the same place, only at a later stage. My beautiful sister passed away in 2019, six years after her cancer diagnosis. She was, and is, the bravest person I know. I miss her every day and acknowledge with gratitude the love and support she gave me in this life. I know she is in an infinitely more wondrous world, and I know that she can be here with me as I write this. Thank you, Jane.

Introduction

Know thyself, for once we know ourselves, we may
learn how to care for ourselves.

Socrates

Sometimes we don't know where to start when we're hit with
life's most challenging experiences, especially when we are
caught by surprise: a cancer diagnosis, a loved one's death,
a desperately sad event, or circumstance that takes us to the
pit of despair. We blunder into it and, if we're lucky, when we
reach the end of it, we find a beginning. We start again — a
new pathway forward, equally filled with joy or challenge, and
made easier by what has gone before.

There is confusion about our pathway forward at first, but
there can also be crystal clarity on the big questions: why we are
here, what have we to learn and how are we to live, really live,
with purpose. Not only is this my experience of cancer; it's also
my journey to spiritual awakening. As I sit here in the evening
light, with the gentle warm glow of a setting sun, and the breeze
at my cheek, I recall a friend saying "there is no but, just and."
It's about learning at the end of any day; and when darkness
begins to fall, remembering our earned wisdom so we can face
the future without fear — and more than that, face the future
with anticipated joy.

The biggest lesson I had from my life and death struggles
is knowing that we go on after death; to an afterlife that is
infinitely and indescribably more brilliant than our earthly life.
Even though there is beauty at our fingertips and wisdom too,
and glimpses of heaven on earth, it is nothing in comparison to
what awaits us in death/rebirth. As I type these words a gentle
orb hovers around my computer, a spirit energy, telling me that
I must continue to write this book, and reminding me that I am

a conduit between this life and the next. I didn't plan for this other-worldly existence, far from the corporate world I built my long career within. In fact, I never imagined that I'd be known as *Maryann from Revealing Light*... spiritual mentor, astrologer and card reader, teacher, and counselor, intuitive, medium, and clairvoyant. This, after 30 years in a fast-paced orthodox career, often at managerial and mentoring level, working for government and business. There are lessons in adversity and in change, and one of the biggest for me has been self-nurturing, boundaries, and the wisdom to say "no," but that is for later in this book.

These days I am not that manager working across the government and business worlds. I am now known across multiple spiritual social media channels as *Maryann from Revealing Light — Tarot, Astrology & Spirituality*.

When I began my spiritual counseling, I had no idea that my connection with the spirit realm would be so real as to be visible to my viewers. Orbs and EPVs are common in the many videos I make on my spiritual social media platforms. I am busy running them these days — long gone are the black suits and white business shirts. These days it's a desk full of crystals, cards, pendulums, astrology charts, dowsing rods and even a crystal ball.

Now, I am variously known on YouTube and other social media platforms, for the many times spirit shows up in the form of an orb, a faery like spirit, or a strange, muffled voice on my video's audio. Sometimes the orbs are round balls of light, shooting across the screen; other times wisps of vapor drifting around me or a light with visible wings. Often, they will dart out from behind me, from my cards as I draw them for my audience and continue to dance in the light of the balcony door behind me. They seem to know when my audience needs a lift or validation. They seem to know when I need a lift and validation. Like many of my dear viewers, death and tragedy, ill health, and pain, have visited far too often in my life. As I channel, they lend their quiet strength, their playfulness and, most of all, their light. People ask me, "what are the orbs in your video?" I answer to the best of my ability:

"They are spiritual energy from the angelic realm; also, my passed over loved ones visiting and helping me on my way, and, sometimes, faery like energy with wings; just as they are here tonight as I write this spiritual memoir."

I can feel my late mother's insistence that I write this book; draw it all together. The cancer journey, the manifestations of spirit in my life, the experiences that we share — you the reader, and I — the channelings and the clairvoyance because these are the gifts that have been present since childhood, not fully understood then and, post-cancer, clearly understood and valued.

I believe we underestimate this part of ourselves, this spirituality, and when we become aware of it, we nurture it and seek to understand and connect with it. When we do this, we find a richness that is beyond anything this earth can offer.

As a young girl, the fifth child in a Catholic family of six children — and the fourth girl behind many "spares," I struggled with my voice. I had so many to speak for me and I wasn't conscious of who I was, where I came from and where I was to go. Looking back on it now, I can see that I grew up with an identity crisis that lasted decades. Internally, despite my lack of self-awareness, there was a small and rebellious voice that I was part of something infinitely bigger than myself — knowing that God or whatever you want to call Spirit, was real and very close. I remember, plenty of vivid dreams, and feelings that there were "others" not of this world close by. I saw them clairvoyantly, sometimes vivid pictures like a movie roll and, at other times, impressions like a stamp might leave on a piece of paper within my third eye. So near, as though I could reach out and touch them and, at the same time, far, far away as if in another world. As a result of sensing Spirit around me (though I couldn't explain what I felt or saw then), and being sensitive to other people's thoughts and moods, I put my focus on animals and nature and it did not, and doesn't, disappoint. I had the luxury of growing up on a farm, rolling green fields, misty blue horizons in winter and orange sunsets and the smell of stubbled wheat fields in summer. I remember being about 12 years of age and, after mustering sheep, stopping on the side of the hill. I'm not sure what happened but I became conscious of the vastness of the sky and the wind about me. I was given the thought, it was a conviction that struck at my core, "know thyself" followed by two thoughts. In knowing yourself, you will know others; and in knowing yourself you will be able to help others. I took these thoughts, or profound messages, and they became beliefs that I would follow over the years, either through often brutal self-reflection or service to others, and a constant searching and learning about spiritualism. Still, I was without that essential ingredient that may have saved me from sadness and much loss. I had neglected to "help myself" or, at the very worst, been misguided about my own needs.

And there it is.

This unconsciousness that retards true spiritual growth and freedom because it's only when we recognize that we are here in service to ourselves as much as to others, that we heal and find our true purpose. You cannot be authentic, strong, and powerful if you've left half of yourself behind.

Later, when I was much older and had completed many years of study, I know that Socrates said "To know thyself is the beginning of wisdom." And the Oracle of Delphi also urges us to *Know thyself*. Socrates in his infinite wisdom takes it further: *Know thyself, for once we know ourselves, we may learn how to care for ourselves.* If only I had recognized that to help others, I must first learn how to help (and heal) myself. For 52 years, I didn't fully understand this task and, therefore, failed at real authenticity. I discovered so much post-cancer, including that inner authenticity is not something that others give you; it is the gift, the reward, and the earned wisdom, that you give to yourself.

And, so, where to begin, dear reader. I must start at the beginning of real awareness, and that came at the time of my cancer diagnosis. It was the catalyst to my spiritual growth and, at long last, the real opening up of my spiritual gifts. First, though, I had to learn to care for, and about, myself.

Part I

A Cancer Diagnosis (2015)

Chapter 1

It's Cancer…

We shall not cease from exploration, and the end of all our exploring will be to arrive where we started and know the place for the first time.

T.S. Eliot

I don't know why we notice the little things when the biggest things are happening to us. It's like we want to be distracted from our reality and be transported away to a safe place of observation. On the day that changed my life, I wanted to stand at a safe distance; to fool myself that it was happening to someone else, not me. Never me.

I remember the paintings in the specialist doctor's office. There was a huge one of him playing a grand piano with his wife. How odd, I thought, that something so grandiose should be in a room where people are waiting for medical procedures, and so preoccupied with what those tests might reveal.

I sat, silently, in that waiting room with its odd pictures, alongside people I didn't know. I remember the very thin, young adult who looked like he was sick, and I wondered if he really was, and what was wrong. Did he have cancer? There was also the fashionably but casually dressed lady with a mess of blonde curls who was curled fearfully around her husband, hands intertwined and leaning close for comfort; the overweight and middle-age lady who appeared nervous, the off-duty businessman preoccupied with his phone — all people waiting for a colonoscopy, like me. When their names were called, they disappeared behind swinging doors. I watched and waited. Back then I knew nothing of what was ahead; back then I was an observer, not central to this story.

And then it was my turn to disappear behind those swinging doors.

I remember waking after the procedure and thinking someone would come and get me up and sensing with a sinking feeling, that no one wanted to speak to me. So, I took the initiative and called out: "Is it fine for me to get up. Did everything go okay?"

"The specialist would speak to me," the nurse said, but I could get up and sit in the chair. Someone came to help me into the day chair where everyone else was eating sandwiches and drinking their tea or coffee.

"Only give her water," the head nurse said. "Would you like me to get your husband?"

"Yes," I nodded, catching the anesthetist looking at me sideways. Not less than an hour previously we had exchanged banter on the way to the procedure room. Now, he was casting furtive glances when he thought I wasn't looking. Why was I the only one in the room who couldn't eat? Why did I feel singled out and alone? What was so terribly wrong that they couldn't meet my gaze?

A growing alarm was ringing. Panic hovered on the edge of my solar plexus. I was no longer the observer sitting in the waiting room; I was right at the center of what felt like a nightmare. I could do nothing but sip my water because my mouth felt so very dry. I hardly dared swallow.

"We'll be sending you this afternoon for a CT scan and a chest X-ray, so you can't eat anything yet," the nurse said.

"Why are you doing that?" I asked a little bit more urgently, as my husband came in with a worried look on his face. Again, the nurse said the specialist would speak to me. So, I waited and tried not to look at anyone in that room, only giving my husband a look that said, "Something is really wrong."

After what seemed like an intolerable amount of time, we were taken to a waiting room. Finally, the specialist appeared. "You have a lesion, a villous adenoma, I've taken biopsies."

"Is it cancer?" I asked.

"I can't tell you, but the odds are 80:20. They're good odds."

"But what do you think?" I implored, hard panic setting in now.

"I can't tell you that, but the odds are very good."

My eyes must have given away my sheer panic because he stood up and said, "Let me give you a hug." I stood up and accepted the hug, such an odd thing for a Professor of Gastroenterology — the one in the grand piano picture — to do.

I stumbled out the door, nearly forgetting to sign the discharge form, and so began the next frightful days of traversing the highway some 200km from my rural home, back and forth, for more tests and poking and prodding, and negotiating cancer diagnosis and medical treatment in a big city. The first thing I did while I was waiting for my husband to get the car — parking is so horrendous in Sydney for a couple from the country — was to ring my sister. Almost to the exact timing, give or take a month, the year prior, I had been trying without much success to console her after she had got a diagnosis of colon cancer. All through 2014, I had walked beside her as she battled her cancer, worrying, crying, disbelieving and then, seeing her treatment and surgery, wondering how life could be so cruel. Now she consoled me.

"It'll be okay. You've got good odds — 80:20. When they first discovered mine, they said, 'It's cancer.'"

I nodded through the tears which were beginning to flow. "You're right. I'll just get these tests done…"

The thing about suspected cancer is that the health system in Australia reacts quickly. This reaction is the same wherever you go, whoever you tell. The word "cancer" sends shock waves through everyone. They imagine what it would be like if it happened to them, and they feel lucky it didn't. Cancer, even suspected cancer, is the loneliest place to be.

After the tests, and an excruciatingly long period of time while I awaited results, I learned that my odds had run out. I was in the 20 percent of villous adenoma sufferers where malignancy is discovered.

Nights were the worst in the beginning. Fear was palpable, like a current running through every part of my body, but mostly in my chest and solar plexus. I was living with electrifying fear. It was that way every time I got more bad news — a running horror movie whirring away in my mind when I was first diagnosed as suspected cancer and, within 10 long days, a definite diagnosis: "You have cancer."

The news sent me into a spin which in the beginning, only ever abated and didn't go away entirely. I had to learn acceptance at that time; accepting that the life I thought I knew with my family, the career I thought I had, and the time that I thought was on my side had all been taken for granted. Of course, in my less fearful and more rational moments, I knew we caught it early, that ongoing symptoms combined with my elder sister's cancer battle a year earlier, sent me to the specialist for a colonoscopy when I otherwise might not have gone.

Once diagnosed, I gravitated towards other colon cancer fighters. When you're around these survivors you know "they know." They know about the symptoms, they know about the pain and shock, and they know what it's like to have long surgery, chemotherapy, and radiation, and be forever changed. Most of all they know what it's like to confront your own mortality, a thing every human being puts off, cloistering themselves in their comfortable existence where being "depressed" means having a problem with someone from work, or a fight with a boyfriend; and being happy is focusing on where they are going "out to lunch" and what they'll eat. Those with cancer taste real happiness at every successful treatment milestone; and real despair when milestones mean treatment hasn't worked.

I looked at these things then and I saw the bizarreness of it, particularly when I saw pictures of a soon to be eaten meal/ selfie on social media. Life revolving around restaurants and café visits shared on social media.

During that time, I began to learn to live in a state of grace and gratitude. Now, food is what I consume to be well, and it will never be a substitute for the real things in life that bring happiness, like love and laughter and listening and talking, giving and receiving; and the most important thing about a meal — the chance to sit and communicate with family and/or friends.

I learnt a lot about "receiving" during diagnosis and treatment planning too. I was supported by family and friends and drew on the wisdom on my sister Jane who, 12 months earlier, had been diagnosed with the same cancer, in the same place. I was shocked beyond belief at her diagnosis back then and tried to help as much as I could, but you don't really know what someone with cancer is going through until it happens to you. And God forbid that it ever happens to anyone else I know and love. I saw her struggle with chemotherapy and radiation, and I was at the Sydney hospital for her surgery. I wondered at the time how anyone could withstand any of this, yet I knew through her inspirational example that it was possible to survive, including the mop-up chemo when your body has had enough of the pain and trauma, and go on because you must; there is no choice, only the hard reality of your diagnosis.

The medicos were shocked to discover two sisters had the same cancer, in the same place. Genetics played such an important part in this familial big picture. I have since found out that while we don't think our parents had colon cancer — Mum passed from pancreatic cancer and Dad from prostate cancer — our extended family on Dad's side did. Our great grandmother and two cousins passed from colon cancer; other cousins were lucky enough to catch polyps before they became cancerous. The trouble is that when we were growing up and into adulthood, the risk within our family was not discussed. What a shame. That is so different now. I have informed my children of the risk because the simple truth is that a medical test can spare you from a lot of pain and suffering, and ultimately save your life.

This is one of the profound messages of this book. Trust your intuition and be proactive about your health. As I look back now, I knew something was wrong in my body, long before I was diagnosed.

Chapter 2

Disconnect

The problem with comprehension is it often comes too late.

Rasmenia Massoud, *Human Detritus*

I felt as though I had done something wrong when I was first diagnosed with cancer, as though I was somehow to blame for getting sick. Perhaps if I had of been more vigilant, focused more on my health and stopped with the "busy-ness," I might have made time for a check-up or given my immune system the hand up it needed. I felt so weak and vulnerable whenever I had to go out socially because with guilt goes shame and I didn't know how to handle all the conflicting emotions I was feeling. I felt different from everyone else, singled out and isolated. I was incapable of normal conversation with anyone other than close family and friends.

I was dreading the appointment with my GP of 28 years, as I walked up that concrete path and into the open-plan surgery, I had so often visited for what now were minor complaints in comparison to cancer; chronic fatigue, a thyroid issue, stress overload.

I had been putting off further testing, despite symptoms for almost a year. However, when my sister was diagnosed in 2014, my GP said I could no longer put it off. And so, I didn't.

I wasn't expecting to be told I had cancer, but who is?

When I was diagnosed, I spiralled down through a combination of depression and fear. I thought back over my life and shook my head at all the times I had stayed back at work too late or let myself be overworked and overloaded. I thought about my constant sacrificing of self for my family, and most of all, for my employers, and wondered why on earth had I not looked after myself. Why, in the ladder of importance, did I put myself on the bottom rung? How could I get it so wrong that I put everyone and everything before my health? What motivated me to dissect petty office politics and extended family squabbles, or carry around someone else's negative energy and unresolved dysfunction?

Cancer is a huge learning curve and the ultimate game changer. You never live your life in the same way. You try and avoid stress and you are choosy about who you allow into your life, and by how much. I will never let myself get overworked again, ever. My children are adults now and it's time for me to live my life in my best interests; to take a bigger slice of life for myself. A lot changed after my diagnosis — for the better and for the worse — and I'll get to that.

Those early tests to confirm diagnosis were overwhelming. I remember being entombed in the MRI machine, the ultimate diagnostic test, the surgeon ordered not long after the results of the biopsy were known, listening to the click of the magnets and fighting off claustrophobia. I pondered hindsight. It could have been so different but as my dearly loved sister Jane always reminded me, how many people say, "Could have, should have, would have?" I supposed she was right; what is past is past. What matters is the now and the journey, the gratitude we learn to make part of our life and, ironically, the cruelest lessons cancer deals us. I now give myself permission to put myself first.

***

The period between diagnosis, while they run the multitude of tests, when they are still deciding the degree of the bad news they will give you, is the worst part at the beginning. It's the not knowing that's excruciatingly frightening for you and for your family. I remember the thoughts going through my mind, that if there is a way out of this, I would take it. Was there a bargain I could make and, if so, with whom? Perhaps this was happening to someone else, maybe they were mistaken? I've dodged bullets before; how could I wriggle out of this one? It was, as you can see, the reactions of a desperate person, slowly sinking into the quicksand of inevitability. To say that this process is a test of strength is perhaps an understatement. Rather, it is brutal, confronting, and extreme. It is a slap in the face with reality that can't be idealized away or wrapped up in some Pollyanna-like positivity. Though, to develop a positive mindset is the goal of the process. Not only must you find the strength you need to survive the treatment, but more than that, the strength to beat cancer. It is a fight for your life and sometimes, for some people, against the odds.

I believe that our strength can be found in the sum of experiences we've had. In those early weeks, friends often said, "But you're a strong person. I know you'll get through this." Somehow those were words I couldn't comprehend because I did not know then that I had the strength to withstand whatever cancer threw at me. How do you know how you'll react today after a day of nausea, to the unexpected impact and setback of treatment, to the trauma of complex surgery and the aftermath of treatment? I drew on my sister's example, that she withstood what was thrown at her and fought so very valiantly. I hoped that I had even half of her strength.

In those early days after diagnosis, each day was a learning experience about who I was, and a test of strength and discipline — disciplining fears and anxieties, disciplining my mind to stay positive and my emotions to stay strong.

Curling up in a ball and bemoaning "why me?" is a downward spiral. There are many mental and emotional routes you can take when you get a diagnosis of cancer. I certainly don't have all the answers, but I do know that you must choose to remain positive. It's the only way to approach it.

I found it easier after the initial fear subsided — not that I lulled myself into a false sense of security — no, cancer sufferers and survivors never have that luxury. It is always present and accounted for, never too far away from the periphery of thought. I suppose my biggest strength remained, as it always was and will be, and that is my faith in something more — God, the creator, an infinite wisdom, and divine presence. This is the same faith that has seen me through the most difficult terrain of my life so far; a quiet but sure knowledge that I'll be okay in the end. But faith must be worked at; it has to be trusted. It's the parachute you have when you take that leap off a cliff and the invisible net you hope and pray will be there before you hit the ground. It's the quiet confidence in a new day and in yourself to sustain, endure and complete the journey you know you're meant to make. Hindsight tells me that like everything else in my life, the people, and situations I've encountered, the work I've been led to do, the lessons I've learned and the person I've become, that cancer led me in directions I hadn't contemplated before. Something so profound and life changing was not without meaning.

Chapter 3

Digging Deep

Never be bullied into silence. Never allow yourself
to be made a victim. Accept no one's definition of
your life but define yourself.

Harvey Fierstein

I wasn't always the girl with cancer, and I'm still not "the girl who battled cancer and, so far, survived." Very soon after diagnosis, I decided I would remain true to who I was. For me, cancer doesn't tell my entire story, and it never will. I am the sum of the experiences I've had throughout my life, including cancer, not because of cancer.

When breaking the news to my friends, who were shocked and disbelieving, I included a caveat: "Be discreet with this," I said. "It's not a secret, but I don't want strangers and acquaintances who have zero understanding of my cancer to lay their reactions to cancer on my shoulders." As a highly sensitive person to others' moods and thoughts, I didn't want their fear or their pity or even worse, "thank God it's not me," though I knew when they were told, that was the hidden thought at the back of their mind.

The other aspect of colon cancer is the lack of education and awareness. I have found there is a degree of stigma when it comes to discussing it. I figured I had enough to deal with, without having to navigate social stigmas too. You might wonder how I can predict other people's reactions to colon cancer? I can because that was the way I reacted before my sister was diagnosed. If it's not something you have to think about because you don't want to contemplate it, then you don't think about it. And that's my point. Everyone needs to get acquainted with digestive cancers, the signs and symptoms, the risks and prevention because colon cancer is on the rise, particularly amongst younger people. Modern-day diets, stress, and the pace of life means we do take our gut health for granted. The message of this book is to be aware, look after your health and never take it for granted.

I began writing this book in real time during cancer treatment to raise awareness and to tell my story of an altered life and spiritual life. It's like me to be an advocate for change even when it's happening to me. Silly perhaps — it's not an easy path — but I believe every experience is meaningful and can lead to change for the better. I've been doing it all my life. As an investigative journalist and later editor, as a public servant with a nose for research and policy options, and as a writer and communications manager working with Indigenous people to raise social and emotional well-being and self-esteem. And now as a spiritual counselor, championing hope for the future, channelings, astrology, and something deeper and very satisfying — validation that life goes on after we die.

I was a good campaigner as a journalist and, later, as an editor of a regional newspaper I won several state awards for leadership and community involvement. One of these successful campaigns was to retain an obstetrician for our local hospital. Without an obstetrician, mums-to-be were transferred to a neighboring town, an hour down the highway, to have their babies. I remember being eight months' pregnant and posing for a front-page photo with other mums-to-be in front of the hospital's maternity section. We hammered the state government so hard that in the end they seconded an obstetrician from the city to our country hospital, at great cost. That obstetrician ensured the hospital was not downgraded and retained a fully functioning maternity ward into the future. To this day, the hospital has an obstetrician, and all mothers can give birth locally.

My second son was born at the local hospital, though my first baby, caught in the politics of rural health funding, was born away from home.

I began my labor at my local hospital but because the obstetrician hadn't been appointed yet, I was transported via a courtesy car to the neighboring hospital. I remember my waters breaking and just wanting to stay at home. This is what it's like for country patients when it comes to health services. It was a similar situation with cancer treatment. There is no radiological unit in my hometown and certainly no colon surgeons. Like millions of other country patients with life-threatening disease, we travel long distances to access health services, and I found myself traversing the highway to Sydney, about a 6-hour round trip daily for radiotherapy over almost 7 weeks.

It evoked memories a year earlier of driving my sister to her radiology and chemotherapy appointments from her local town to a larger regional center, a two-hour, one-way trip — or four hours' driving, each day.

During the daily drive to Sydney, I had my laptop, and I wrote. It's what I knew and it's how I had channeled my voice for decades. I'd been a professional writer most of my mainstream career and writing about my cancer "journey" helped put me in an observer's role, allowing me to step outside my painful reality at the time.

I like to think I've been lucky in this life. I've mostly always been able to be in the right place at the right time. I've pushed my career ambitions while being a mum to three sons, and a wife and partner. I've worked in a big city and nationally in a variety of roles from journalism to research and policy, and communications management. I've worked at the forefront of Aboriginal affairs in Australia and have never once lost my passion for good journalism, and good writing. I've prided myself on my learning and being able to acquire new skills and seek out new professional and personal horizons. And I've always found a haven in my family, nature and in spiritualism.

In fact, I've devoted a good many years to researching spiritual knowledge and have been innately drawn to subjects as diverse as the healing power of nature, intuition and psychic ability, alternative medicines and modalities, energy work and life after death. I suppose in all my querying I was seeking to understand the mortality of my loved ones after experiencing the passing of my parents, and my own mortality. To understand death, though, you have to understand life.

However, I didn't think for one minute — not one — that I would be confronted with cancer. Cancer treatment is not for the faint hearted. All pretense of modesty falls away as you realize you simply have no choice in the indignity you will likely have to endure in treatment, surgery and examinations. You are rarely in control of events.

There is nothing redeeming about cancer that I could see then. And now? It was the spiritual awakening I'd always signed up for. It was a complete and utter 360 that led me to realize spiritual gifts, particularly clairvoyance, that had been dormant since childhood.

Back then, though, it was testing times. Uncertain times.

As I waited for my treatment to start that took around two and a half years to complete, I again fell back on faith. Of course, it would be okay. Of course, I would come through this and move onto a better, richer, more meaningful life, understanding as I must that there are no guarantees and if you fail to listen, then the lesson will meet you, blocking your path until you understand.

Chapter 4

No Good Choices

It's hard to fight when the fight ain't fair.

Taylor Swift

There's nothing fair, or kind for that matter, about cancer. In my experience, it's an absolute bitch. I remember seeing my sister suffer through chemo/radiation and confronting invasive surgery. She then backed up for five more months of chemotherapy without complaint. She did it to survive because she wasn't ready to leave her children and husband. She did it because, as she often said, "you've got no choice."

She fought for six years, until she couldn't fight anymore — until there was no choice left but to let herself slip away, having been told there were no more treatment options left.

I understood her fight logic back then. Cancer doesn't play fair at all. It lays before you a grueling and painful regime and once completed, it's never really finished with. There is the nerve-wracking three-month CT scan to make sure the cancer is gone at the end of treatment, or worse still, hasn't spread, and then there are the three-monthly blood tests and six-monthly CT scans, and yearly scopes. You are only considered cured beyond five years because this is the terminology the medicos talk in. They marry staging up with five-year survival rates. One thing I would suggest to anyone diagnosed with cancer is to stay away from looking up the five-year survival rates. It will do you no good and just create fear for the future.

I chose instead to interact with my Facebook group and to take note of the many survivors who were into their sixth year or more being cancer free. They were the veterans of the war against cancer and in each one you will find nerves of steel and, most of all, a strong positive attitude and love of life. The commonality is they go on living their life without cancer being front and center all the time. They work, they play, and they exercise and look after themselves nutritionally, and in every other way possible.

Everyone battling cancer knows you need resilience to get through the treatments and surgery.

"It changes you," my sister said to me when I told her I would not be putting up with patronizing attitudes from anyone involved in my treatment. "You become quite strong, and you don't hold things in anymore. You say what you need to say and that's a good thing. I bet that by the time you're finished you will be very strong and not take any nonsense from anyone. And that'll be a good thing because you have been too soft on people who don't deserve it in the past."

I thought about that. "I don't know. I hope I get a bit stronger..."

"You will. I know you," she said.

And you must be strong because dealing with cancer makes you hypersensitive to anyone who doubts what you've pinned your hopes on, and that is, you are hoping for the best possible outcome. My first experience of how hope can be shot down was from my radiologist. A practical man of science, he began our first consult by expressing his doubt that I could have the difficult operation I wanted, rather than an alternative surgery which would have been even more radical.

By this stage, I was getting a little impatient. He was, after all, not my bloody surgeon.

"Look my surgeon is confident he can do the operation."

The radiologist clasped his fingers together in front of him. "So, my job is to shrink this tumor," he said.

"Well, that's why I'm here," I fired back.

This simple exchange sent me spinning back into the fear response and depression that characterized my initial shock on diagnosis. He doubted it could be done! I would wake up in the morning on the verge of shaking with what felt like an electric current of fear running through my body. I had nightmares of giant cranes crashing onto nearby buildings while I was running for my life to escape the debris. In all my dreams, I was far removed from anything or anyone I knew, alone in an alien landscape.

My sister pulled me back from the worry, again.

"He's a radiologist not a surgeon. Why would you take any notice of him when your surgeon said repeatedly, he can do the operation?" she said.

"Yes. I know. I suppose. It's just he was so negative about it."

I spent days thinking about it. The truth was that I'd been at the hospital when she'd had her operation.

I could hear her nodding on the other end of the phone.

"Perhaps you know too much," she said.

"Maybe."

In the end, time worked its magic. The fear lessened and I looked forward with hope.

Chapter 5

Treatment Begins

Don't you dare.
Shrink yourself.
For someone else's comfort —
Do not become small.
For people who refuse to grow.

Unknown

The morning of my treatment began rather dramatically. I woke to the sound of a savage thunderstorm; deep, thunderous booms and a dark and overcast sky. "Typical," I thought. The morning of the day I have to swallow chemotherapy tablets and get zapped with 45 Grays (radiation measuring term), the heavens decide to send the wrath of God to my home. I lay in bed, the safest of all places to be no matter what's going on. I simply didn't want to get up. I briefly had the "why me?" thought and just as quickly dismissed it. Nothing, I thought, was going to change my dilemma. I had cancer — or as I preferred to refer to it, mutating cells because cancer is such a scary word — and that was that. The time for prevention had passed.

I rolled over and listened and watched. I didn't need to get up immediately and so I rested in the middle of the storm. As I did, I looked out over my balcony to catch the magnificent sun beginning to break through the clouds. "Anything is possible," I thought and reached for my phone to snap the moment. I would post the photo on Facebook with positive words for my family and friends, to signal to them that I was ready to face my treatment and, for those who knew I had "mutating cells," that if I could go into this day with positivity then they could too, no matter what their dilemma or concerns.

As we drove down the highway on Day One of my 44-day chemotherapy/radiation battle, I switched on my e-reader. I had downloaded a book called *Radical Remission* by Kelly A. Turner. In this book, there are nine commonalities that cancer survivors — those with incurable cancers — have. These common factors include radically changing their diet, which I had already done before I read the book. It was just acting on what my "gut feeling" was telling me. I cut out 90% of dairy except eggs and hard cheese (my favorite). I removed too much red meat from my diet and increased fresh fruit and vegetable intake. I eliminated refined and processed food and tried to eat the freshest of ingredients. The other instinctive elimination was sugar. This was a drastic change for me, given I had a self-declared sweet tooth.

Another commonality was embracing supplementary therapies. While I hadn't consulted a naturopath or herbalist since diagnosis, I had increased meditation sessions and consulted a Chiron Healer who provided energetic healing sessions to remove physical and emotional blocks.

Perhaps the biggest ah-ha moment in reading the book was the chapter on releasing suppressed emotions. Boy had I failed in this department. Looking back over the long years of subjugating my own needs to others or putting up with a situation long, long after its use-by date, particularly in the workplace, I began making new rules. They say cancer is a great teacher and I agree.

I would describe myself as a sensitive person, emotional by nature, inclined to be introverted and, when a situation becomes too tough, I tend to subdue my voice and go within. How utterly and diabolically stupid of me. For decades I had let bullies and other people's agendas "dumb me down," all because I feared confrontation and, worse, consequences. I realized on that highway, traveling to my first date with chemo/radiation therapy, that I had inadvertently been living in fear: fear of losing my job and not being able to provide for my family, fear of not gaining the approval that I mistakenly thought would authenticate me, fear of losing what I considered critical relationships, fear, fear, fear. And yet, here I was with a diagnosis that provoked fear, taunted it and said, "beat me and you will live." Of all the things I had been fearful of in the past, this was the big kahuna.

Chemotherapy was tough. So was radiation. Before you even start, there are multiple people from the nurses to the doctors telling you about the side effects. I heard about radiation side effects from no less than four people. Chemotherapy side effects were repeated by three people on three different occasions. You receive so much information (presumably to get your informed consent to the harsh and potentially life-threatening treatment), that if you thought you might be safe from side effects before you spoke to the medicos, you sure didn't by the time you took that first tentative step through cancer therapy center on Day One.

As usual, it was my sister's voice of reason that penetrated through the cold waters of the fear I had begun to sink into. "Look, don't say 'when,' say 'if.'" You may not get any side effects and automatically thinking you will, is not good for you. When I do this, I can jinx myself, so say 'if.'"

"But if I think about the worst-case scenario then when it's not, I'll be presently surprised," I countered.

"These side effects might not even occur, and I know you will worry about things, and it doesn't take too much before you're feeling down," she said. "But I also know that you are a Rogers (my maiden name), and you have the strength of the Rogers. You will get through this."

Something clicked. I remembered my father and his quiet countenance when things got tough. How he faced his prostate cancer — which later went to his bones — with quiet resolve, and how when he fractured his hip and was lying in his death bed, he was concerned about us because we had been sitting in the room too long. "Go home," he would say, "I'll be okay."

I thought about generations of Rogers, and I believed that I had inherited their strength and then I thought about the incredible will and resolve of my mother. Those same strengths had meant that I sometimes achieved the impossible. My sister was right. It was time to put fear to one side and get on with the job of healing those damned "mutated cells."

Chapter 6

Signs of Support

The quieter you become, the more you can hear.

Ram Dass

I was raised a Catholic. My family sat in the same pew every Sunday at Bulla Creek Church — a small, wooden church in the middle of nowhere, set amidst eucalypt gums, and grazing sheep and cattle. The church was a Sunday ritual for the many farm families in the area. We'd get dressed in our best clothes so we could hold our own with the other families and gather around the social conversations after the service. While it was an opportunity for my parents to mingle, in truth it was a bit of a non-event for me. I found church long and boring and couldn't wait to head home to the menagerie of animals I'd collected on the farm; all of whom shared many an adventure with me.

While church did little to convert me into a religious devotee, it did introduce me to the mystique and the power of spiritual ritual and prayer. Later in life, I pursued knowledge and awareness of all types of spirituality from eastern religions to Zen, and from psychic phenomena to paganism and Celtic spirituality. In the end, I settled on a combination of all that I had learned, only sculptured to fit my own individuality, my own soul space.

When I was diagnosed, I began to see white feathers everywhere. My research into spirituality — spiritual guides, told me that when you were going through a tough time, or in need of protection or divine help, then a white feather signifies that you are, indeed, being watched over.

"They're everywhere," I said to my somewhat, doubting husband.

"Well, of course they are. There are white cockatoos everywhere this year," he countered.

"But they're always in my path," I persevered.

"Because you are looking for them."

"I'm not…"

"You are."

And so, the skepticism went, but I knew as sure as faith steers you "miraculously" in the right direction sometimes, that the numerous white feathers were for me. One even turned up right in front of my chair, *inside* my house.

My meditation teacher called. "I just wanted to let you know that I have something for you."

"Oh, okay. What do you have?"

"I was collecting the mail and I had a thought about you and your sister and then, as I turned to go inside, there was white feather right in front of me. I nearly stepped on it. I knew it was for you and it's here when you want to collect it."

When I went to Sydney for an appointment with my surgeon, there were four white feathers in front of my steps as I walked down the street. Countless, and constantly, recurring examples of divine help. As I said, they were everywhere.

Still my husband remained skeptical until the day we were driving along the highway enroute to my Sydney appointment with the radiation machine. Out of the air, or on a breeze, came a white feather, directly in my path to meet our car which was traveling at 110kph. It sailed right through the air to me and hit the front window.

"Wow, did you see that feather?"

He nodded, thoughtful.

"It's like in the Forrest Gump movie," I said. "I wonder where these white feathers will take me?"

He smiled, still not conceding his skepticism but I knew somewhere he was thinking about the meaning behind coincidence.

Thank God for the signs and symbols that give me comfort; that made me think that I wasn't alone and there was a divinity that might just be keeping an eye on me. I hoped and prayed because chemotherapy and radiotherapy at the same time, or separately, are not a walk in the park.

***

The chemotherapy had side effects by week two. Depending on how much rest I had and how well I managed them, they were endurable but unknown and frightening. At the end of week two I had a bad night with pain in one foot and leg — hard to describe — but an ache in the front of my leg, extending deep into the muscles. I panicked, thinking it might be a thrombosis but pushed through the dark of night to morning without needing to make an emergency dash to hospital. By dawn it had quietened down to a dull ache in my ankle that eased as the day wore on. To be on the safe side, I walked that afternoon and kept moving as much as I could around the house. By day's end I was confident that it was only an example of the aches and pains that people describe in their legs during chemo, but it reminded me of the seriousness of what was being pumped, and beamed, into the living tissues of my body.

I read on my online cancer support site that "chemo isn't for sissies." One fighter had a sore mouth virtually from Round One of chemotherapy, weakness in the legs and a lot of anxiety from wondering whether she was going to be struck down with any more of the horrendous side effects they tell you about before you begin.

I found that all my specialists accentuated the side effects, though I know they needed to do this for informed consent. The side effects of radiation were horrendous to contemplate but worst of all, a sarcoma cancer that could develop in about 20 years.

"I need to point this one out because you are relatively young for cancer and it might surface in your lifetime," the radiologist said of the potential for sarcoma cancer.

The side effects of chemotherapy were equally daunting: hand and feet neuropathy, nausea, diarrhea, mouth ulcers, fatigue and, at the extreme end of the scale, thrombosis, heart attack and stroke.

I heard these side effects repeated, and I saw through my cancer fighters' group just how many of these side effects actually happened. Okay, so it may have been one out of approximately 600 members who needed to be intubated but that one person's story was enough to frighten anyone beginning chemotherapy.

As I've said many times before, the thing that helped me was remaining positive, gathering the information I needed to make the right decisions and listening to my "gut feelings." I had also begun to use nutrition to help manage the effects of the toxicity I was experiencing. I had actively researched nutrition's ability to heal and I had begun to trust my "gut instinct." As well as teaching me about pain and dealing with fear, I was also learning to listen to my inner voice and to trust it.

But the best laid plans often go awry, and we're forced to pick ourselves up, dust ourselves off and start again, even when it's the last thing we feel like doing. Week three of chemo/radiation therapy came around and so did the predicted side effects — with a vengeance. They hit on the weekend and wrought pain and deep fatigue. By Monday I was saying to family, "Some days I just can't fix it, no matter what I try and what I do. Those are the bad days."

The truth was that my body was fighting one hell of a battle to rid my system of the cytotoxic chemotherapy and the powerful and burning effects of the radiation. I prayed each day that the conventional medicine I had chosen to undertake would kill the cancer, while my own efforts at doing everything I instinctively knew was best for me — nutrition, meditation, positive thoughts and feelings, and faith — would get me through.

Often, I counteracted the onslaught of side effects with a warm bath. It soothed and refreshed. As I lay there, I began to think of times past when cancer was the furthest thing from my mind. As I plotted our upcoming Easter egg hunt, a tradition in our family, I knew I wouldn't be participating this year. Just as I wouldn't be going out to lunch with my friends in the foreseeable future. Chocolate hunts and food feasts held no appeal despite the opportunity to make them into an occasion for family and friends. I have always been a person that creates with gusto, whether that is a firelit supper, a hearty roundtable family breakfast, a movie marathon, a picnic, or a walk amongst the sunlit pines near our house.

I love drawing attention to the specialness of the moment, and I've always had an eager audience in my family. As the only female in the house, my boys often use the word "random" to describe me, and I'm happy with that. Never predictable but spontaneously enthusiastic, I love to create the atmospheres within the home that my children, partner, and friends deserve, and that I deserve. It has always been my pleasure to create and experience the joy of creating for others.

Normally, I would be looking forward to Easter festivities, including the religious ceremonies in our local cathedrals but this Easter I knew I would struggle.

"I'll try making a light cocoa," I said to my husband.

"What, no Easter eggs?"

"Not likely," I said, "but I'll try the cocoa and make it for everyone for brekky."

Lying in that warm bath, staving off the nausea and stomach cramps, I cursed the cancer. Nothing would be the same again, I thought. My work would change; my spontaneity would dampen; what on earth would I be capable of after treatment?

"Bloody cancer," I said to the four tiled walls of my bathroom. I was happy I was alone with my thoughts because I knew my family needed me to be positive. I thought about my youngest son, in the bedroom next door, and studying hard for his HSC midyear exams. I should have been bringing him a cup of tea and a snack or helping him study. Instead, in the most important year of his schooling, I was lying in a bathtub hoping that the tablets held, and would continue to hold, to give my inflamed body a chance to heal.

It was times like this when all normality deserted me that I wondered about the future. "Please God, let me survive this so I can live the best life I can," I spoke to the empty space around me, hoping that my prayers were being heard.

**

My husband picked a pink flower for me the next day on the trip back from radiation, when we stopped off in a quaint town in the heart of the Southern Highlands, about an hour or so from home. It was the sort of thing a little boy might do. It was a delicate pink and I know designed to make me feel special. In his eyes, I guess I was, though I felt anything but special unless you count special enough to get cancer.

Chapter 7

Fall Down, Get Up

Fall seven times, stand up eight.

Japanese Proverb

I found it harder and harder to get out of bed in the early morning as we traversed the highway daily and the radiation and chemo effects began to snowball. I was desperately trying to manage them in the last three weeks of treatment. I was quickly becoming exhausted by what my body was enduring and the constant traveling. Some days, I doubted whether I would see the treatment through and I was beginning to understand the real meaning of that old saying, "one foot in front of the other." I was no longer taking assertive strides into my treatment but desperately holding on.

The list of side effects was growing. I was tired all the time, and it was a fatigue no sleep could fix. The pain was, at times, excruciating. The fatigue they said would strike before the end of treatment was no understatement. The burning — radiation goes in and comes out, so areas around the tumor site burned and throbbed. Radiation treatment is tough but there is nowhere to run to and hide; you have to keep going with it to get the hoped-for result. And then you combine that with the side effects of chemo, nausea, and more fatigue. By the end of six and a half weeks, I was a mess mentally and physically.

I normally have a strong and controlled mind. I don't fall apart, but by week five I was starting to fray around the edges. Each day I traveled down that highway with my husband at the wheel, was a day that I surprised myself. I never knew when I went to bed for my usually disturbed night of sleep whether I would be able to get up in the morning at 7 a.m. and make the trip. I was constantly fatigued and in pain.

I took the nausea pills they gave me, along with the six cytotoxic chemo drugs each day. I got to the point where I detested food but ate to keep taking the chemo which had to be consumed with food. The kilos literally melted off and by the end of the six and a half weeks, I'd dropped seven kilos. It's not a diet I would recommend.

By week six I was wondering how I would survive. I slept mostly on the drive down the highway, during that last week and a half of treatment. On the Monday, at the beginning of that week, I was drifting off by the time we got halfway, when a voice inside my head uttered two words: "higher stasis." What on earth did that mean, I thought to myself, but this wasn't the first time I'd received a flash of insight from, seemingly, out of nowhere. When I got home, I looked up "stasis." The dictionary defined it as "A state of stability, in which all forces are equal and opposing, therefore they cancel out each other; or in medical terms, a state in which the normal flow of a body liquid stops, for example, the flow of blood through vessels or of intestinal contents through the digestive tract."

I didn't know it at the time but it was clairaudience; it was certainly not the first time I'd experienced it but during treatment, it was pivotal.

"Okay," I said to myself. "Perhaps this meant that if I slept often enough, I would not only slow the digestive tract down, but also give the body a rest from the radiation onslaught." I cultivated sleep, wherever and whenever. I slept in the car, I slept while I was waiting for the trusty radiography technicians to come and get me — I slept in the afternoons, and I went to bed as early as I could. I quite literally slept my way through week six and the last two days of treatment that spilled into week seven. I don't know how much it helped, but I do know that while I was asleep, I wasn't in obvious pain.

I came and went from the cancer therapy center like a zombie, barely noticing my surroundings, that is, until I was waiting to see my oncologist and was sitting opposite a breast cancer fighter. She was surrounded by two breast cancer nurses in their pink shirts. They were devoting all their attention to the lady. This was good for her, and I remembered thinking, as I was sitting by myself, "why are there no colon nurses here?" It was a question I couldn't answer.

I had plenty of support from my sister, my good friends and my husband during these tough times and I drew heavily on that, and my own instincts. I learnt a lot about managing digestion during the worst of my treatments, through diet. One of the timely interventions by the radiologist, who had turned out to be very supportive after all, was a referral to a dietician.

"You sound like you're doing well with your diet, but we can take it back even further," the dietician said.

"Further, but I'm eating white (low fiber) everything," I countered.

She basically recommended the BRAT diet: bananas, rice, applesauce, and toast. It's the diet doctors might prescribe when you're recovering from a stomach bug. It includes "binding" foods. These are low fiber foods, and bananas, which are high in potassium and help replace nutrients the body might have lost.

She also recommended avocado, spinach, and plenty of mashed potato, and if I were to eat other vegetables, to remove the skins where the highest fiber was found. I began eating plain crackers with avocado for lunch and chicken breast, potato, and spinach for dinner every day. While she recommended cornflakes, I soon worked out that cow's milk was causing pain and discomfort, so I switched to almond milk and added porridge instead of cereal. Porridge, I discovered, like avocado, was a soluble fiber rather than an insoluble fiber and if you have a digestive system undergoing harsh cancer treatment, you want these gentle but nutritious foods. Between the dietician, my instincts and trial and error, I was able to control the impact of chemo and radiation just long enough to get through the end of the treatment.

I finally reached the end of treatment and walked out of the cancer therapy center feeling like I'd just been released from jail.

"How long until the side effects subside?" I asked in my final review with the radiography nurses.

"About two weeks," she said, "and they may peak before they subside, but by the second week you should be starting to feel better. We will ring you at the end of the first week and the second and, if for any reason you feel you need to, ring us. We are here."

I nodded, grateful to finally be leaving that big, rotating machine that fired its radiation rays and did God knows what to me and, hopefully, shrank the tumor.

"Thank you," I said, eager for the conversation to be finished and to get into the car for the last trip back home. Although it was the end of my treatment before surgery, I didn't experience the lift in mood I'd anticipated. Rather, everything seemed bleak and non-life affirming. Hard to explain, other than to say that my usual Pollyanna-like enthusiasm for life had got up and stomped away, leaving me heading for the depression that took two days to arrive.

The first day after treatment ended was blissful. I didn't care about the side effects; they would soon abate. I even managed to potter around the house, tidying bedrooms, putting washing away and making previously neglected rooms look inviting. I felt halfway normal that first day only to plummet into the depths of depression on Day Two. It followed a particularly rough night, where I was up and down because of the radiation's impact on my bladder. There was pain and pressure in the radiation site, and I contemplated taking painkillers. I tossed and turned and by early morning's light, I wondered if I would ever feel comfortable and normal again.

"Maybe this is as good as it gets," I thought, with just a touch of defeat in my heart.

It was that thought and with a massive surgery in front of me, that led me to desperately reach for my phone and begin to google "easy ways to take your own life." My fingers froze over the keypad. What was I thinking? Instead, I called my sister.

"Not a good day for me," I said in answer to her usual, "how are you going today?"

"I'm feeling really down and thinking what's the use of going through all this. Maybe it would be better…"

"Come on," she interjected. "Now don't be so silly. You'll get through this. One step at a time. You'll be okay, like me."

I had to stop and think then because the truth was, she was okay back then. She'd been driving over to see me for the day, whenever she could, and I often thought that she looked better than she had done in the past decade.

"I know. I know. I'm just being silly. It's just that getting through treatment occupied all my thoughts and reserve and now I'm lying here in bed, looking out the window at the autumn leaves falling and wondering if I'll ever feel normal again."

"It's the low that comes after treatment. I had it too," she said. "It's normal to be feeling the way you are. Hang on, and I'll be over to see you on Friday."

She did come on Friday, and we spent a good deal of the day laughing at our own jokes. It worked well to diffuse my low spirits and to remember that things would get better soon.

"You've got one big step out of the way, and now onto the next big step. The surgery," she said.

I looked at her in total understanding. I remembered her surgery only too well. "I might have to be taken kicking and screaming through those operating doors, you know," I said.

She was quick to reply with the right direction. "You won't. You'll do what I did, chat to the staff; make jokes with them. The thing about the surgery is that the cancer will be taken out and it is the biggest step done and dusted. And you have no choice, and you just get on with it."

I nodded. "In a way, I'm looking forward to the surgery because it means the cancer will be gone."

She smiled. "See, you've gone from kicking and screaming to looking forward to the surgery that will get rid of your cancer."

Thank God for my sister. I doubted I would make it through without her.

Chapter 8

Light in the Tunnel?

Sometimes your joy is the source of your smile, but sometimes your smile can be the source of your joy.
Thich Nhat Hanh

It was a soon to be wintery afternoon in May, 11 days after I finished the hardest treatment I've ever done in my life. During the first week after my radiation/chemotherapy, the side effects did lessen but it was often one step forward and two steps back. By the second week, as the radiology nurses predicted, I was starting to see the light at the end of a very long tunnel. I had one good day, followed by a bad day and then two good days in a row. My joy was uncontainable, simply because it reminded me that life can exist without pain and discomfort; that those relaxing feelings can run through your body and not get mown down by the shrapnel left behind from cancer treatment. My inflammation was easing. I even tried a little hummus on a biscuit and tolerated it. Such is the joy in the simple things when your body and mind had been under fire for almost two months.

It began a thought process. If I could turn this thing around in 11 days, then maybe my recovery from the operation wouldn't be so bad.

The operation. Major surgery loomed large on my not-so-distant horizon. It was the biggest thorn in the crown, the curative treatment, the toughest of them all. My surgeon didn't mince words in telling me how tough it would be.

"It's major abdominal surgery," he said, "with complications ranging from blood clots, heart and lung complications, sepsis, and infection. So, you want to cross your fingers."

Cross my fingers, I thought. Hang on a minute, he was the expert. He must have picked up my wide-eyed terror because he corrected himself. "Look, I've done hundreds and hundreds of these things and most of my patients are okay, but it is major abdominal surgery and I want to stress that. You'll have a nasogastric tube as well."

My heart sank. It was one of the things I didn't think I could handle — think tube being inserted through your nasal passages, and down your oesophagus to your stomach. Terrible visions of the tube getting stuck down my throat surfaced. Have I mentioned I'm also claustrophobic?

He also pointed out that I would be cut from the top to the bottom of my torso. Major abdominal surgery, I thought with horror.

When I arrived home from that appointment, the familiar fear took hold. "Can I do this?" In the waking hours, that fear gripped in my solar plexus, and I huddled close to my partner in the dead of night. I suffered with night-time terrors as a child and that was how I felt, like my worst nightmares had come true. It took me a couple of days of floundering around mentally, wondering if I could overcome the fear. I thought at one stage pills might help, and I contemplated asking my GP for a prescription, but knew that would only be a Band-Aid solution. What I had to do was find a way to conquer the fear. Easier said than done, but I tried. Every time the fear feeling gripped, I would begin to push it away and imagine myself walking out of that hospital post-operation, well and cancer free and able to go on with my life. I focused on the words of my surgeon. "We are going for curative here." I remembered I was reasonably early stage and for this stage of colon cancer, surgery is considered a cure. If surgery was my biggest hurdle in this cancer battle, then I would meet it head on.

One of the most therapeutic ways a cancer fighter can spend their time is getting back, as much as possible, to normality. As a result of cancer, most fighters are housebound because of the chemotherapy or recovery from surgery. Chemotherapy lowers the immune system and so going out into large crowds and exposing yourself to infections and viruses is potentially quite dangerous. If your immunity is low, then you have nothing to fight with; that's why oncology will give you a card to say you are on chemotherapy which is designed to fast track you through the Emergency Department.

"If you get a temperature, go straight to ED," the cancer center nurse told me before I began my chemo, "and show them this card. You'll get triaged straight through and most likely be put on prophylactic antibiotics."

Believe me when I say that the benefit of going out for a cup of tea (I didn't drink coffee for years during and after my treatment) and a muffin to a café is so very insignificant when compared to the risk of infection. So, we stay indoors and watch the days slip by, isolated, and with time to think about the survival statistics or our next treatment, or how sick we feel. That's why a little bit of normality goes a long way, like a friend coming over for a cuppa and a chat or a walk.

As the time wore on, though, I was able to hold my fear of the operation in check by getting back to normal, or as close as I could get to it. For the first time since diagnosis, I felt a little like my old self when I rang my hairdresser who had a home salon and booked an appointment. When I walked into the salon, I really didn't know what to say, but it didn't matter. My hairdresser is a lovely, kind, and generous soul who let me tell my story about cancer in any way I wanted.

I told her that it had been a hell of a year, that I'd just been through a hell of a treatment, and I was exhausted and needed rest. "But coming out today to get my haircut... well this is a highlight. Thank you."

Something as simple as a haircut gave me more pleasure in social interaction than I had had since diagnosis. I looked at myself in the mirror, as my hairdresser gave me a new short "do" to go to hospital with: "So it won't need to be styled," she said.

The reflection staring back at me was animated. The eyes were smiling, though tired. I looked for a short time, like I used to look and for just a moment I forgot that I had cancer. For cancer fighters and survivors, thoughts of cancer are always on the periphery. That reflection made me think about the mental, psychological, and spiritual value of learning to go on with life; of living bravely by not dwelling on cancer. I'm not advocating denial, but I am advocating the value of getting on with your life once treatment has finished. I wondered what that would be for me, and my spirits began to lift. There would eventually come a day when my treatment was finished, and I felt certain that day was not some distant and unrealistic hope, but a concrete fact. I have much to give back, and I intended to help as many as I could through their battles with real and genuine understanding of what tough times mean.

That reflection was a small glimpse of the strength that was possible to take away from my cancer experience.

But at the end of the day, when you are alone with your thoughts, or its 3 a.m. and the familiar fear re-engages, the need to work hard to overcome panic and anxiety is palpable. My biggest fear during the 6–8-week recovery was the impending doom and gloom I felt around my surgery. No matter what I tried, I could not get my head around the five-hour operation. What would I be like afterwards? Would there be much pain? How could I control possible complications when I had no choice but to succumb to the surgery? I simply had no answers, only fears.

And I still couldn't control the irrational — or was it rational — fear that penetrated upon waking. It was like there would never be another day that I could wake up optimistically until after the surgery.

I began reading. I googled my surgery and found out as much as I could about it, I spoke to others who had the same operation and comforted myself that they'd made it through. Eventually, I turned to the familiar tool I'd always used to move forward, books. I downloaded Dr David Servan-Schreibere's *Anticancer: A New Way of Life* book, and I downloaded Ian Gawler's *You Can Conquer Cancer*. I began meditating (as suggested in both books) to try and become more positive; to snap myself out of my fear and to calm and orient my mind. Of course, I was focusing on the worst-case scenarios, something that I've always done to try and shield myself from the worst, but this wasn't the way to deal with my fear this time. Rather than logically examining the potential outcomes of the surgery, in my head I was rehearsing my goodbyes to my children. The waves of anxiety were truly consuming, until I began to meditate three to four times a day. I began to use imagery as well, and affirmations, techniques described by the Australian cancer warrior Ian Gawler whose story of curing himself of an incurable cancer is one of the legendary tales anyone who's had anything to do with cancer knows about. Gawler, funnily enough, was quoted in the US based *Anticancer* book, such is the infamy of his work with cancer.

The meditations helped, and I began to visualize myself healing well from the surgery. I began to read positive and inspirational stories of people running marathons with a stoma (mine was temporary) and living life to the full.

I used healing essences on my solar plexus to banish away the fear and I substituted positive thoughts for negative, but at the root of my inability to control my fear were my old enemies: stress and anxiety — two unwelcome companions that had dogged me all my life. In fact, I believe that the effects of stress had indirectly led me to a cancer diagnosis, and that was something I had to face and conquer.

Chapter 9

Grief Impacts

Where'd the days go when all we did was play?
And the stress that we were under wasn't stress at
all just a run and a jump into a harmless fall.

Paolo Nutini

My earliest memory involves my mother being chased across a moonlit and barren plain by a zombie. That dream scared the living daylights out of me and caused me great anxiety by highlighting that my number one carer could be taken away from me. I was around four to five years old at the time and my mother says I woke up screaming in terror. Yes, my mother could be potentially taken away, but it also burnt a deep fear in my psyche — that there were unspeakable terrors in the world and that I may have to face them alone.

As I grew up, I learned to stretch the boundaries of safety to experience new things. I was always hellbent on acquiring knowledge, so I often didn't stick to the safe path. I left home on the farm for the "big smoke" as we called it then (Sydney) when I finished school and worked there for four years before backpacking overseas. When I returned from my adventures, I enrolled in university and completed a Bachelor of Communications, majoring in journalism and English. My first post out to a regional newspaper meant I was in the right place at the right time (many would argue differently — said with tongue in cheek) to meet my husband, Eric. Three sons later, I had established my heartfelt dream: to begin the next phase of my life as a mother.

When the boys were old enough, I went back to the newspaper and eventually became its first female editor. This was also my first experience of chronic stress and its impacts on health. I was a successful editor, raising circulation and increasing revenue, and winning industry awards for excellence. One award meant that I beat 44 male editors for the NSW Country Press Award for editorial writing. Editing a newspaper was instinctive; I absolutely loved starting each day with a blank slate and an idea of what the publication might look like once the stories and photos were filed. I assembled each edition with care, often working late. Then it would be home to bathing babies and toddlers, assembling dinner, putting on numerous loads of washing and keeping the house tidy. It was no wonder that I got glandular fever, followed by its cousin cytomegalovirus; both viruses rendering me too exhausted to move and ended with a bout of chronic fatigue syndrome. I knew I had to scale back to something that was less stressful. Unfortunately, passions often lead us into peril, and it was with great sadness that I gave up journalism to take up a government position with more structured hours, or so I thought back then.

But just like the little kid who overcame her fears to push the boundaries, I grew into my role of communications manager and then senior policy officer with the government. It was a privilege to serve, and the national focus was never lost on me. I traveled across the country in my role, talking with farm families, community leaders and their service providers. I got to put my thumb print on research, policy and program development and I made firm friends during my almost eight years in the public service. Again, I made the mistake of working too long and too late and neglecting my health. I developed fatigue and heart palpitations and was later diagnosed with an acute deficiency of magnesium that was "enough to hospitalize the normal person," my doctor said. At the same time, my body was battling an overactive thyroid condition called Graves' Disease. All the while, I was commuting each day — a three-hour round trip. It was time to eliminate the stress of the travel and so I took the offer of a position with an old newspaper colleague and friend working in Indigenous affairs, again with a national focus. I wasn't to know then that this move would throw me into one of the worst years of my life and provoke untold stress, grief, and sadness — all in the year preceding my cancer diagnosis.

***

There is an anecdotal commonality in cancer fighters' stories if you listen closely enough. It is usually a tale of great stress and strain sometime in the year or two prior to cancer developing. It can be the death of a loved one, great financial stress, divorce, or some other estrangement with a relative, a job loss or a combination of all these things. The stress usually lasts months and takes the individual beyond their normal coping mechanisms. They feel overwhelmed for a sustained period. This major stress, where I struggled to keep my head above water and literally felt I could not cope, occurred in 2014.

The year began with my sister's diagnosis of colon cancer that sent me into a spin. Surely something so horrible could not happen to a loved one. I remember crying in my office and wondering if I was going to lose her, but with true grit she made it through her major surgery. My old newspaper colleague, friend, and boss, Gavin, was understanding and sympathetic, and was generous with the time he gave me off when I was required to look after her. It was a busy start to the year with plenty of projects and responsibilities. I was heading up an online publication with junior journalists in my care; at the same time, I was writing communication strategies for government, managing the business's public relations activities for numerous products, and was writing feature stories across two magazines, as well as editing one of them. I had again begun to think that I was working too hard and too long, particularly with the added personal worry of my sister, coupled with the difficulties of raising teenagers.

At that time, a new conservative government had taken power. We were almost entirely reliant on government funding and many Indigenous organizations were experiencing funding cutbacks. My friend and boss didn't seem worried about the political climate, even though I was concerned. I had heard the political rhetoric that there just wasn't the money in the government coffers for services that were not "frontline." Our services were outreach and cultural. I had also been in touch with my old colleagues from the public service who were predicting across the board funding cuts to many programs.

As the new government budget date loomed closer, we were notified that funding in the new financial year would be cut. The products and services we delivered, some built over 20 years, were all defunded. It sent my friend into deep depression and anxiety. He was forced to make his 32 mostly Aboriginal staff redundant. He was given just 20 days' notice to close everything down before funding ceased. He often said during those days that it was "one day for each of the 20 years." I was one of the last to go and on a bleak Friday afternoon he called me aside.

"We've done some wonderful work together; it's been a great ride," he said.

I looked at him sideways, wondering what he was getting at. "You're shutting the business down? Everyone's being made redundant?"

He nodded.

"I'm going to be rattling around this big old building by myself," he said, trying to stifle tears.

I shook my head. "No. I'll stay and help you pack up and we'll shut the door together in six weeks."

Downcast and beaten, he left that night. It was mid-morning on the Saturday that I got the call that he'd hanged himself.

***

To say I was devastated by the death of my old friend was an understatement. The outpouring of grief, the understanding of what a tragedy his death was, reverberated across the nation.

On the Monday we all assembled back at work, heartbroken. It was my job to manage the national media attention, all the while trying to keep speculation that it was the government's fault, controlled. I did this because that was what he wanted. We had been working on a public statement about the funding cuts in the weeks before his death. It was my responsibility to release that statement that night. It was a gracious statement, so typical of my friend, who'd always been loyal to the government of the day, particularly the public servants. This stemmed, in part, from his own early days in the public service after he left the newspapers — experiences he never forgot when he was tasked with delivering programs for government.

The statement thanked the government and those public servants who'd helped him over 20 years and the Indigenous and non-Indigenous community who'd supported his organization. Despite the pressure to blame the government, I announced that the statement was the only one we would be making. I fought off many journalists in that week, trying for a cheap headline. I knew the tricks of the trade, of course, and used this knowledge to rebut, defend and resist. Uppermost in my mind was to protect his memory, his work and, ultimately, his legacy.

All that week the national attention was excruciating; and then there were the calls from Indigenous people who were angry and grieving. Not only was I trying to manage my own grief but also the grief of others. When I look back on that horrible, horrible time, I realize that none of us should have been working that week, that what had happened had shocked us to the core, and we should have been let go to grieve. It didn't get any better in the weeks and months that followed.

The administrators were brought in, and we were given our notice. By the time we were finished in September, we'd spent some three months in a building without time off to grieve, that was nothing more than a shell compared to its former life, in offices next door to the big main office where once my friend had loomed larger than life. It was beyond sad, and I never want to go through something like that again. It was, quite simply, sustained, acute and overwhelming stress. The kind that cancer fighters might refer to in the year or two before their diagnosis. For months afterwards I struggled through grief and anger, both with my friend for taking his life, and at the government for destroying so much that was good, and real and working. That is the nature of suicide, a fermenting pot of emotions, at once so hard to comprehend and understand, and, for me, in a way, to forgive.

By February 2015, I had received my diagnosis. The tests had been prompted largely by my sister's cancer diagnosis but also because I just couldn't seem to bounce back from a dreadful tiredness that sapped all my usual energy.

I remember wondering then, as I saw an uncertain 2015 stretch into the future, would life ever return to normal? But it did go on, interrupted by the grueling regime of chemotherapy and radiation.

***

Life between the end of radiation and chemotherapy and my "curative" surgery wore on and the weeks passed between me trying to shake off radiation induced fatigue and building up my fitness levels again for surgery. Unfortunately, the seasons in my hometown decided to take a turn for the worse and early winter conditions prevailed. I have never felt the cold so intensely before. I longed for the sunshine, prompted by the wonderful memories of seaside holidays on the coast. Most weeks, we also had rain. The skies were overcast, the landscape dreary and wet, and I was chilled to the bone — a hangover from chemotherapy. Although we had the fires roaring, I just could not get warm.

To add to my doldrums, I had lost all vestiges of an appetite. I was dropping a kilo a week and I had a lackluster outlook on mostly everything that had given me joy pre-diagnosis. Was I suffering depression? At times, possibly, but overall anxiety and fear of the future were my biggest issues.

When you are diagnosed with cancer, your life — or the life you thought you had — stops. You are thrown into a kind of limbo, particularly if you have to give up work for treatments, which a lot of cancer fighters do. Giving up work leads to financial worries, so cancer fighters often have to contend with the whole basketful of challenges that life can throw out, all at the same time. And there isn't a lot of help readily available. There are no colon nurses available to co-ordinate care between the end of treatment and the wait for surgery. Co-ordinated care, though not specifically colon, existed at my cancer therapy clinic for the period of my treatment but not to manage lingering side effects afterwards.

The waiting for surgery; the anticipation of what was in front of me, tested every coping mechanism I had. The ever-present specter of cancer, still in my body, loomed like an encroaching darkness on my horizon.

As the gray days threw their chains around me, I continued to meditate to alleviate the anxiety, imagining that a healing white light was shrinking my cancer and that my body was healed. I rarely ventured into the outside world, other than to visit a few trusted friends. I kept in touch with life through my social media feeds, regularly visiting my online support group. It helped to interact with people who had, or were, battling cancer.

Without work to occupy my mind, without the extra money to spend on social outlets, with the threat of cancer to my health, our finances and future, including my longevity as a mum and carer for my three sons, I sank into a routine that consisted of sleeping, eating because I had to, a little housework and cooking, and my one big daily achievement: walking the dogs on a gray afternoon.

It became hard to remember who I was. Always the strong one, always setting goals for the future; the person to lean on in troubled times. I felt helpless and, very often, hopeless against the onslaught of the cancer. It was a huge wrecking ball that had come into my life, demolishing most things I took for granted, including my future, or at least that's how I perceived it in the waiting time before surgery. I couldn't even console myself with an endpoint because the endpoint was complicated, risky surgery.

When the surgeon suggested I undergo an Endoscopic Ultrasound prior to the main surgery, I shriveled up inside.

"Why?" I asked, wide-eyed.

"Well, I want to see how well the radiation and chemotherapy worked and I don't want any surprises when I get into the operation," he replied.

"But I'm still feeling the impacts of radiation," I said, knowing it was useless to argue. The surgeon, in whose hands I was placing myself for my main surgery, wanted another test to complete the picture before I was on the operating table. I nodded instead.

"Okay, but can we please leave it two or three weeks."

He agreed.

I got the call from Liverpool Hospital in Sydney. The procedure would be held a little over three weeks after I'd finished radiation and chemotherapy. Yet another prep to do, and yet another time when I would hand my body over to the medicos. Again, I felt the rush of helplessness. There truly was no escape from what was in front of me. I did what I'd always done since diagnosis, I attempted to steel my mind, shut off the anxiety, and find a pathway through to positivity.

"It may throw up some good news," I said to my sister. "Maybe the tumor has shrunk."

"Yes, Mare, you have to find the positive in everything."

"True, but it's hard going."

I dug deep to find the strength of mind to get myself to Sydney when all I wanted to do was sleep and stay warm, rather than undergo another procedure. I wondered how my system would take the prep, and I gritted my teeth for the inevitable pain that would flare again in my already traumatized body.

The test went well, and as it turned out albeit performed under general anaesthetic. I was out of theater in just over an hour and on my way back home that afternoon. The results weren't available immediately, but my body was already telling me that the tumor had benefited from the radiation.

As I reflected on my operation, I knew that for a long time I'd missed the signals my body had been giving. As I went about my busy days, with my mental to-do list, eyes firmly on the series of rigid mini-goals I'd set myself — which now seemed insignificant, pointless even — I had numbed myself to what I was physically feeling. As I had pushed myself towards achievement in the workplace to mask the real problem; insecurity and low self-esteem, I had unwittingly sacrificed the opportunity to be in touch with my body. Had I been listening, it was telling me to slow down, rest, speak up and set boundaries. I had lost my will to take care of myself and, for a very long time, the will to "do right" by myself. Everyone else was getting something from me, whether at work or even on the home front, and there was nothing left for myself. But playing the martyr is dishonest. The truth is that I was not taking responsibility for myself. Set boundaries and mean it; and you gain self-respect.

This was one of my great regrets since diagnosis — that it took cancer to lift me out of my self-induced fog. How simple the truth seemed: *Listen to your body and address what it is telling you. There are no real barriers to good health except the ones you are creating and perpetuating.*

I have a lot of dear, dear friends, made in the workplace and socially over several years. Once I make a friendship it is for a very long time. I treasure my friends, but I also worry about them too; particularly the career-oriented mums who try and do too much with too little time. It's obvious to me from my own experiences trying to live up to the ideal of the "super mum," that neglect can lead to ill health and, worse, disease. Here is my ideal daily to-do list with the benefit of hindsight:

- Relax, slow down and breathe when you first wake up in the morning. Remind your children of the rules: beds made, showered, dressed and school bags packed by the time you get to the breakfast table. Teaching your children self-responsibility will enable them to be functional adults and that is a goal worth setting.
- Yes, you can walk out of the house with dishes in the sink and washing in the laundry. All things can wait until you can do them without rushing.
- Work needn't consume you. You are not building an empire but working for a living; not living for working. There's a difference. Don't overload yourself and set boundaries. It's just as important to do this at work as it is at home.
- If you work through your lunch hour as a rule, you're a schmuck. Rather, eat a healthy lunch and put your gym shoes on and go for a walk.
- Take five minutes at afternoon teatime to relax. A day at work does not have to be done at breakneck speed and you'll be more productive if you have regular, short breaks anyway.
- Knock off at your knock off time. That's what it's there for; it's the end of your paid work for the day. Don't leave

your family out on a limb waiting for you to get home. They deserve more than that.

- When you do get home, don't attempt to give the house a makeover as you're walking through to your bedroom to get changed. Do one thing at a time and delegate some chores to your family. Devote the next hour to doing something you want to do, not have to do. You subjugate your will when you aren't following your passions.
- Don't waste time watching a soapy serial until 11 p.m. just because you are "mindless" at the end of the day. Instead, make some time for meditation, contemplation or physical relaxation. Examine your needs, listen to your body, reflect and, most of all, nurture yourself.
- If your body is trying to give you a message, get yourself checked out. Don't put it off until your holidays, or a week when you're not as busy at work. Act on your gut feelings, don't ignore any doubts and be proactive with your health. Even though you can't see it now, it will make a difference.

I wish I had enacted this list on any given day over the last 20 years, particularly the last five years when I think my health took a nosedive. It might have sent me for testing earlier and I might have avoided major surgery, but there it is again, pointless regret. The real trick is to learn the lesson well, and finally.

Chapter 10

A Big Surgery

To escape fear, you have to go through it, not around.

Richie Norton

As I sat in my GP's surgery waiting for my appointment post-Endoscopic Ultrasound, I noticed the Cancer Council of Australia's pamphlets on colon cancer. One pamphlet was headlined: Colon cancer kills more Australians than breast cancer. I wondered why they would make that comparison in a pamphlet. Could it be that to draw attention to the high incidences of colon cancer, the cancer council drew upon a highly publicized and prevalent cancer, breast cancer?

The day before I had been on the phone to the cancer council for a follow up survey for their program "Cancer Connect." I told them I'd been happy with the program and would recommend it to others.

"Having the opportunity to talk to someone who has been through what you're going through, same cancer and same treatment, is invaluable," I said.

"Would you be interested in volunteering yourself once treatment has finished? We usually leave you alone for about 18 months, but we really need more people like you because we had to bring someone from interstate for you," the cancer council person said.

"Sure. Of course. If it helps someone else in my position, I am more than happy to volunteer."

That short conversation told me that colon cancer support and resources were outstripped by demand. National, high profile awareness campaigns were only just kicking off in Australia. Countries like England appeared to offer more co-ordinated campaigns with clear targets to raise awareness of the need for screening and prevention.

Australia was beginning to act but it occurred to me that while we had the massive breast cancer awareness campaigns — we were dealing with a "sleeper" when it came to colon cancer. Not only were the stats high, and just a little frightening, but more and more younger people were being diagnosed. Just like breast cancer where a 25-year-old may have once been dismissed by their local GP as too young to have the disease, so too were people in their twenties with symptoms not considered for colonoscopy to investigate potential colon cancer.

The time for a sustained and high-profile public health campaign on colon cancer and screening was here and, in an ideal world, perhaps 5–10 years ago.

I was lost in these thoughts when my GP called my name. He looked tired and appeared to have aged overnight. As it turned out cancer had touched one of his family members and we spent the first half of the appointment talking about our fears and anxieties. I left his surgery again thinking that cancer is indiscriminate; it targets randomly, regardless of age, and it never fights fair.

My GP urged some abdominal wall strength building exercises. "It will build your strength so that recovery from the open, abdominal surgery will be easier."

I nodded, and when I got home began gentle stomach crunches. With my surgery less than a month away it was imperative I build my fitness. The operation, with all its risks, loomed on my horizon. I was doing all I could to prepare, physically, mentally, emotionally, and spiritually. In my mind I was trading off the risks with the chance to rid the cancer from my body and begin my journey back to good health.

I researched and spoke to people who had been through my surgery and treatment. I tried to find out as much as I could about the things that scared me. It was a way of taking back control, and it helped with the treatment decisions I was making.

While cancer once struck absolute terror in everyone, with treatment now more people were winning the fight. Cancer was no longer a death sentence, and I began to strengthen my conviction that I'd be around long into the future. I pictured myself post-surgery beginning a gentle walking program again. I pictured myself doing simple things again, knowing the cancer had been removed and how relieved I would be — perhaps for the first time in six months to know two of the most difficult medical milestones had been met.

"You will meet those medical milestones and tick them off and soon your cancer will be a distant memory," my friend who had been cancer free for more than 10 years said, "but you will be fighting this for most of this year."

"I know. It's a year out of my life but one day I hope to be like you; well and truly having moved on and living a normal life."

Inspiration came in small packages: like the long conversation with my GP, or the generous responses from my Facebook cancer fighters when I posted questions on all aspects of my cancer journey. Or when I turned to my husband and said: "I'll be alright, won't I?"

He looked me squarely in the eyes. "Yeah, you'll be alright."

Or when my sister patiently went through my fears one by one. Or the anaesthetist at the hospital who kindly said he would give me a pre-med (a light sleeping pill) in the ward before being taken down to theater to ease my fears. I had real and tangible support but at the end of the day, when night had fallen and I was in my bed drifting off to sleep, the ever-present specter of my upcoming five-hour operation loomed.

I noticed that I was overreacting to the slightest drama, or negativity; my coping mechanisms were virtually zero.

I couldn't watch the news if there was an accident report, or someone had been assaulted. I couldn't speak to acquaintances in my life about their dramas — normally I was the "go to" girl for some off-the-cuff counseling. I refused to socialize in the lead up to my operation, except with tried and tested good friends. I could be honest with them and tell them that most of the time I was scared witless.

It came to a head one day as I was driving to visit a friend. As I was temporarily reliving the worry-free feeling of how it used to feel visiting my friend in January, before I knew I had cancer, I realized I couldn't live immersed in fear. On the spot, I decided to stop researching my operation, and my cancer in general. I knew enough; I didn't need to spend hours obsessing, gathering information and asking myself "what if." I was incapable of controlling the outcome of my surgery or life beyond that. It was in the hands of my surgeon. Instead, I asked myself, "is your surgeon experienced and competent?" I knew he had impressive credentials and my enquiries had found that he was regarded as someone "who knew what he was doing."

There was also something bigger at play. I always had faith in the universe's plans for me before diagnosis. I should now cultivate the belief that I would survive my surgery, meet my challenges head on, and beat cancer. I wanted to stop focusing on the fear and I wanted to let go of my need to control the outcome. I had to put that in the hands of my surgeon, and in the hands of God. And so, I got off the cancer sites and filled my days with long walks, television, reading and writing. Pottering and being easy on myself. I literally abandoned my fears to the universe. I let go and gave it over to faith, trust and a belief in something bigger than myself.

I had always liked the "Serenity Prayer," something that alcoholics get to know intimately. I found myself thinking of that first verse:

God grant me the serenity
To accept the things I cannot change;
Courage to change the things I can;
And wisdom to know the difference.

I knew that I had done all I could to influence the outcome of my battle with cancer. The waiting game, as the days rolled by, was nearly at an end.

The night before the operation, my two sisters came to stay at the same motel as my husband and me. It was a difficult night knowing that surgery was scheduled for the following morning. Saying goodbye to my sons as I left home that day for the Sydney hospital, was even harder. I had discreetly left instructions with my eldest regarding the family heirlooms and looking out for his brothers.

"Why are you telling me this?" he asked.

"Well, I could be laid up for quite some time and I just wanted you to know…"

He looked at me strangely but did not take it any further because that would have been to acknowledge that the surgery I faced was major and carried risks.

I was instructed to arrive at the hospital at 8.30 a.m. Saying goodbye to my husband and sisters before I entered the pre-op doors, was also extremely difficult. I drew on an old technique I used to use before public speaking which normally terrified me; I'd done the preparation and as much as I could do to influence the outcomes and there was no point in worrying. In the hours that I waited alone in the ward before theater, I numbed myself and withdrew into a calm space. I didn't need the pre-op sedative, instead opting to stay alert before theater. As they wheeled me into the operating theater, I knew that the only thing I had to hold onto was trust in God that I would make it through.

***

My earliest post-operative memory was the excruciating pain that gripped my lower back and pelvis. I vaguely remember swearing at the registrar who'd been summoned to tell me I had been given pain relief.

"Well, it doesn't $*&*ing feel like it," I said.

This pain was worse than childbirth; worse than anything I'd ever experienced. I'm not sure what action they took but mercifully I descended into unconsciousness and woke again, numbed from the pain this time, back in the ward with my hand on the buzzer that released a steady morphine dose. Relatively stable, I was able to consciously realize I'd made it through what turned out to be a six-hour operation. With drips and drains hanging from my arms and body and a catheter and nasal gastric tube in, my options for movement were limited. Despite that, I insisted on getting up the next day and walking. I slept a lot and, when they removed the nasal tube and I was put onto a light diet, I attempted to eat the most nutritious of the food served despite having no appetite. Somehow, I knew that nutrition and walking when I could, would be the keys to my recovery.

I'd like to say my time in hospital was restful, but the truth was, recovering from major surgery was no walk in the park. Another cancer fighter who'd had the same operation told me that her surgeon had likened our operations to major heart surgery in invasiveness and recovery time.

For the entire six days I stayed in hospital, my blood pressure was low and my heart rate high, reflecting the seriousness of the operation.

When I was released home, I found I hardly had any energy to talk or move, nursing an abdominal wound that didn't heal easily. I began to wonder if I would ever feel well again and if I'd ever be free of the horror movie that was my life post-surgery. My back muscles ached if I stood for any longer than five minutes. My stomach muscles felt like they'd been kicked and punched; abdominal nerves caught and tugged, and my insides felt like they'd been stabbed. It was a slow, painful, and stepwise recovery.

Thankfully, my body began to heal with good nutrition, supplements, and plenty of rest. My wound eventually began to heal, despite an infection caught in the hospital, and when I felt well enough, I began gentle walking: 100m, then 250m, then 500m and 800m. My next goal was a kilometer which I reached at six weeks. I intended to build back up to three kilometers a day, which was what I was doing daily before the surgery with a couple of bouts of interval jogging in between. I hadn't missed out on reading the numerous research studies that advocated exercise to help prevent cancer and recurrence.

Like most post-operatives, I didn't leave the house except for medical appointments. Managing the pain and the healing meant that my confidence had plummeted to an all-time low. Rather, I focused on the pathology report that was completed post-surgery on the tumor they removed. I read and re-read it every second day. My cancer was slow growing and non-aggressive. It wasn't in the blood supply or lymph nodes and there was no macroscopic invasion of the colon's muscularis propria — in other words, it hadn't gone outside the colon wall. It appeared I had dodged a bullet. It was a result I had wished for, hoped for, and it strengthened my faith in a benevolent universe; that perhaps I had more life to live. I was luckier than some cancer fighters and I reminded myself every day when I visited my online support group of the Stage IV fighters who have not been so lucky.

As my body began to heal, I had longer periods without pain. I remembered what it was like to feel normal, to live without the specter of cancer. Despite the long road back to full health, I allowed myself to see a glimmer of light in that long tunnel. As

I pounded the turf on my walk, knowing that the clink in my hip would eventually go, and the muscles in my back and torso would eventually strengthen, I allowed myself to be a little less fearful and more confident in the future. Time would tell and, for the moment, it was my friend.

Chapter 11

Recovering, Surviving...

Cancer is like a teeter-totter. Sometimes you gotta go down to go back up.
John Kennedy, colon cancer survivor

As the weeks passed with my wound healing and my body in less and less pain, there were mornings and afternoons when I began to feel almost normal. I made the most of these times because they reminded me that although my body had been altered forever there could be normality just around the bend, and that's what I craved. As I pushed myself to walk daily despite the cold of my hometown winter, I did so with the knowledge that getting more and more active would give me back my physical independence.

On those cold, overcast days that I walked, I continued to think about self-responsibility and how I would attain optimum health in the months and years ahead. I had been lucky. With a bit of luck and maintaining good health, I'd be around to experience the rest of my precious life.

Gratitude was an emotion I actively cultivated on those walks. I was grateful to the universe and to a benevolent God, spirit, Buddha — whatever name is comfortable for you to consider — for allowing me to embrace life with the chance of longevity. Of course, I always live with the specter of the cancer returning, but I was grateful to come through and to have a prognosis I know other cancer fighters, diagnosed at a later stage, didn't have.

At the six week point I knew I needed to confront the question of whether I would need more chemotherapy. I hoped I didn't, but I rang my cancer therapy clinic and asked what my next steps might be.

"The pathology report diagnosed me as stage 2a," I told the nursing co-ordinator. "Surely, I wouldn't need any more chemo. They don't give chemo to some stage 2a cancer fighters."

"Look, that's wonderful," the co-ordinator said, "but that will be the oncologist's decision to make, and you will need at least one appointment with the oncologist."

"Okay," I said, "but I'm sure I won't need any more."

I felt my body had been through enough. I had seen how powerful the immune system could be with my wound healing and what happens when it isn't functioning well, and I was acutely aware that chemo kills off the immune system. When I rang-off from the nursing co-ordinator, though, I knew that if they offered me mop-up chemo as a treatment that would give me even a five percent chance of beating the cancer for good, then I'd take it. Mop-up chemo, if I needed it, would be my insurance policy. I only hoped that my early staging would mean I didn't.

While I waited for my oncologist's appointment, I tentatively accepted an offer to go back to work. I had mixed feelings, mainly because my body was still healing but the truth was, I desperately needed to get back to normal. Even a semblance of normal would do — that was what I told myself in those early wakeful hours of the morning.

So much of cancer puts you on the sidelines of a "normal" life, but it's equally true that so much about cancer means you live life with more meaning than ever before. In those early hours, and sometimes those early morning dawns, I thought a lot about what it means to "live." Before, I'd only ever got to glimpse that joy in living. Now I could see it. I was up close and personal with life, living every moment in the knowledge of my mortality. Cancer does that; it makes you appreciate the moments.

"You look so well," a long-time friend and former workmate remarked one day while visiting.

"What do you mean? You're not the first person to say that to me. Gosh even my GP said that the other day," I said.

She frowned, trying to think of a way to describe it. I interrupted.

"So, I look better now than I did before the operation. That is what they all say. Is it because I look less burdened?"

She took her time in answering. "You look like you are moving forward... recovering and I don't just mean from your operation. You also look like you are moving on from the horrible events of 2014."

I prompted even further. "Yes, that is all true, but I also believe that cancer casts a shadow over you... perhaps one that those closest to you can subconsciously perceive. Perhaps the 'burden' I carried was a 'knowing' that something wasn't right with me. Cancer, or any health crisis for that matter, is one of the most climactic events that can occur in a lifetime."

After she left, I began to think more about how well I looked. It was true. The whites of my eyes were clear which accentuated their greenness. My skin was free of blemishes and dark shadows. I had lost about 25 kilos through treatment and surgery, so I was at a reasonably normal weight for the first time in many years. Sometimes, I would be filled with an absolute joy in living that felt like it began in the soles of my feet and made its way to the top of my head. I radiated health and vitality. I was glad I was alive.

Returning to work was a no brainer for me. My previous employers were willing to give me two days a week as a permanent part-time employee, working from home: ideal conditions for someone recovering from cancer. Of course, I couldn't turn it down. The trouble was, that it coincided with a general increase in my activity levels and that, combined with one long day at the computer, followed by two half days, sent me spinning back to the pain levels I had endured in the days following surgery.

I managed to get through to the 11-week post-op mark before I visited my GP to ask for a renewal of my prescription for painkillers. I had been on them immediately post-op but had valiantly weaned myself off the pills, far too soon as it turned out.

"The muscles burn," I told him. "It's really painful. What's causing that?"

He looked unperturbed. "Look, mate, it wasn't just your abdominal muscles that were cut during surgery but all the nerves too. These nerves are waking up; beginning to heal. Some are finding new pathways and are firing and misfiring. That's what the burn is all about; that, and you are no doubt overdoing things."

"Possibly," I admitted. "How long till the burning stops?"

"Oh, it varies. You know, you and I aren't as young as we used to be. In some people maybe three to four months."

"Okay, then. I'm 11 weeks so I've still a month or two to go," I said.

"Perhaps, it's hard to tell. Have some patience. You will get back to normal. There will come a day when you don't have any pain. Be patient."

I nodded. It was hard, this being patient, when the pain was ever present and stopping me from getting back to normal; reminding me that I was in treatment for cancer and not like everybody else. I just wanted to be independent, to not have to rely on my husband for simple things like grocery shopping because I couldn't carry bags, or vacuuming and washing the floors because I couldn't do that either or carrying a clothes basket to the bedrooms to put the washing away. There were any number of things I did without thinking before that I could no longer do, and it frustrated and disappointed me.

"Okay," I relented. "I'll be more patient, and I'll try not to overdo things."

"But you look so well," he said, as I moved toward the door.

I smiled. Yet another person who saw the absence of cancer in me. I wondered how I would go on chemo if I was offered it. The appointment with my oncologist loomed and I knew that, ultimately, I would have to decide on whether to go ahead, or not. I wondered how well I would look in the months ahead on chemo, as it sapped what was left of my immune system that pre-surgery radiation and chemo might have destroyed.

Chapter 12

Mop-Up Chemo

If you are going through hell, keep going.
Winston Churchill

My appointment with my oncologist couldn't come soon enough. I needed to cover all bases and if I had to have chemo, then get it started. Unfortunately, the appointment coincided with a three-day writing workshop in Canberra. I was undecided whether to attend and had a myriad of questions running through my head: How would my fatigue and pain levels go? Is it too soon to be venturing out in the world after what I've been through? In my usual "just do it and think about it later" fashion, I accepted with the proviso I would need to leave early on Day One of the workshop to visit the oncologist.

The workshop was the second part of a program which I was lucky enough to attend in May, earlier in the year. That first workshop coincided with the end of chemo/radiation, and I was exhausted and fearful of my upcoming operation. I remember I felt different from everybody else, and exposed. Exposed because I had to tell them I was writing about my experiences with colon cancer (I was writing this book back then). I remember seeing the shock in some people's faces; I also remember the pity and their thinking "glad it's not happening to me." I also remember some judgments, "do they know what caused the colon cancer." I repeated often that my family was genetically predisposed to this cancer, but still I felt, or imagined, judgments.

The truth is that while these are risk factors, colon cancer generally does not discriminate. It strikes at the super fit, the vegans, the gym instructors, the health food store owner, and the naturopath (yes, I have met these colon cancer fighters); and it strikes at the very young (unfortunately there was a 22-year-old on my online support group page).

So, it was with great relish I decided to dress like my old self for the second workshop. This time I was cancer free. I put on a dress and a black jacket the first day. I styled my hair and wore makeup. I looked like I used to look going off to the office. When I arrived at the workshop, I lost count of the participants who remarked how "fabulous" I looked. Whether it was the extra effort I'd taken with my dress, or some of that joy in living that I exuded, I felt at home at the workshop and not different at all. I left early on that first day and made the 1-hour trip home to see the oncologist. Arriving on time, I sat in the waiting room in the fading afternoon light, hoping he would say I didn't need more chemo but perhaps knowing that I might. He was more than an hour late, but I didn't care. A kindly cancer volunteer chatted with me to pass the time until 5.30 p.m. when she went home.

"Do you want a beanie or a scarf," she said.

I shook my head. "No, I won't lose my hair as I will probably be on chemo tablets again."

"Oh, that'll be good." She didn't sound convinced.

It was around 6.15 p.m. when I eventually got to see the oncologist. He didn't make it easy for me, leaving the decision up to me.

"I would normally offer someone at your clinical stage chemo," he said.

"I was downstaged in the end," I protested.

He countered. "But that was after chemo/radiation. I look at what the MRI tells me before your operation."

I didn't mean to argue; I just wanted to get the factual reasons why I should do chemo and not just because it was prescribed as a matter of course.

"Okay, then what are the advantages of me having chemo," I asked.

"It is difficult to say because it is unclear what benefit someone at your stage gets from chemo. We can say it will give you a 5% increase in your survival rate. There is also an added risk of metastases with your cancer. At the end of the day, if you can live with a decision not to have mop-up chemo, then you might decide not to have it."

I began to have that sinking feeling that I would most likely have to have more chemo. But he was a reasonable person and genuinely wanted me to decide for myself.

"What does your gut feeling tell you?"

"That's a bit unfair," I said, "I am fearful it will recur."

"You have very good pathology," he said, "it's unlikely."

I thought for a few minutes. On the one hand 5% could mean the difference between life or death. When I was diagnosed with a villous adenoma before the biopsy results revealed cancer, my gastroenterologist gave me 80:20 odds, that is, a 20% chance it would be cancer. I had told myself I would be in the majority not the minority. Unfortunately, I'd been wrong. I wasn't going to leave anything more to chance.

Eventually I said, "I was hoping you would suggest a compromise."

"That was what I was going to suggest. How about we start it and if the side effects are too much, we can always stop it."

"That's what I was hoping you would say," I said.

I left that evening with mixed feelings. Chemo is tough treatment. I felt my body had been through enough. How was it going to cope with a new assault in an already weakened state? I had the required blood tests which revealed normal cancer markers. I was relieved. My liver function tests and lymphocytes were not normal, reflecting the months of treatment I had undergone. They weren't so far out of range that they wouldn't start the chemo, so on a sunny morning I picked up the tablets and listened while the nurse went through a series of questions including my end of life plans.

"Do you have a care plan for end of life?"

I looked at her in amazement. "What is an end of life care plan?"

"Things like, do you want to be resuscitated; how do you want to be cared for, at home or in hospital..."

"Why would you ask me those things?"

"I'm sorry, it's just in the form but you do need to think about these things, everyone does."

"Well, I don't know..."

"Just think about them, okay, and we can talk about it later."

I nodded, eager to be out of that oncology unit with those dreaded pills. I hurried home. I wanted to take the first dose — the sooner I began, the sooner I would finish and tick that elusive tick box on my year-long treatment regime.

I longed to do the things I'd taken for granted before cancer, like sitting for longer than an hour without pain, or attending an all-day workshop without having to leave halfway through because of pain and burning muscles, or fatigue. I wanted to be physically strong again.

The first days of chemo were marked by nausea and fatigue as my body grew accustomed to the poison I was deliberately ingesting.

It was Day Nine of Round One that I began to feel uncomfortable, aside from the nausea I'd had since the first few days. It was the tiredness that no sleep could fix, waking with nausea and stomach cramps in the middle of the night. That told me the chemo effects were cumulative and, as I looked at the pack my pills came in, I began counting down, hoping quickly to get to Day 14 to have a week off, when, hopefully, I would feel better. I wondered what the next five rounds would be like, over four months.

By Day 11, I felt downcast. I was conscious of my disabilities — I couldn't lift the wood into the fire and if no one was home with me, I would freeze. I couldn't get up from the chair for extended periods — if I was in the house by myself, I would feel isolated. There was pain still in my abdominal muscles when I overdid things, and the random shooting internal pains that made me wonder whether the cancer was, indeed, gone. I hated being so debilitated. I had taken being strong, feeling strong in my body, for granted. When that strength and ability is taken away, so is your freedom.

I had been doing well before chemo, aiming for progress, but chemo put me back to square one. It's hard to describe to anyone who hasn't been on chemo, but it's a feeling that you're slowly killing your body. I wondered what my blood tests would be like before Round Two — most likely not bad enough to stop it, and nor did I want to stop it either. I would hang on for as long as I could but the day that I finished, seemed like the holy grail.

That is the thing with cancer. It is so easy to become negative, downhearted and to lose hope that one day life will be good again. So easy to look at others who are well and wish like hell this had never happened to you. So easy to resent the ease at which others go about their life. To know that they did not have to think about an onslaught of pain; nor spend months incarcerated in their home because of the disabilities cancer delivers.

On Day 11 of Round One of chemo, I hated my life, and I was tired of the pain. I was bitter and cynical about cancer and its cruel treatment. I was nowhere near recovered from major surgery and still I was ingesting poison daily.

All these thoughts on Day 11 of chemo. Inescapable prison bars across the window of my mind. No blue skies and sunny, yellow daisies for me. Instead, the harsh reality of what had happened to me; what could happen to me.

It's easy in the post-apocalyptic world of cancer to become downhearted. God, bring on the blue skies again, I thought, but I knew I'd be better tomorrow, or the next day. I knew my hope would return and my motivation. It was just bloody chemo.

***

By Days 12 and 13 I'd got back on the horse again, only to be derailed by severe pain on the night of Day 13 and on Day 14. It took my breath away and worried me; should or shouldn't I go to the Emergency Department? I opted to stay at home and by the evening of Day 14, I was in bed just after 9.30 p.m., sleeping soundly. Relieved, I managed to eat toast for breakfast and enjoyed a cup of tea. Halfway through my breakfast I reached for the medical pack that housed my pink chemo pills and realized that I had a week off from the grueling regime. I nearly jumped for joy. As the day wore on, I began to feel better and by the evening was looking forward to food once again.

I had been working two days a week, beginning nine weeks after my operation. I logged on at 9 a.m. and went to work, doing what I've always done, writing, conceptualizing, and strategizing. It took my mind off my chemo worries and before I knew it, it was time to clock off. Despite work adding another complexity to withstanding my treatment and recovery, I firmly believed it would be beneficial in the long run, not just financially but to my general well-being and remission.

I believe in the power of the mind to heal. It's a belief that goes back to childhood and my mum who had a strength of mind I've rarely come across again. For better or for worse when my mum made up her mind, all else (and everyone else for that matter) followed, including her physical health. She was able to successfully live with very high blood pressure right up until it eventually contributed to her death at 81 years of age, via a heart attack and, later, a diagnosis of pancreatic cancer.

As a child I used to love going to her bedside table which was full of very interesting books. One book caught my eye and, to this day still resides in my memory as an indicator of one of the more surprising aspects of my mother's personality. It was a book by a Chinese author on the power of the mind to influence health and well-being. I remember being surprised that my mother, a registered nurse, would have a book by a Chinese author given I hadn't even heard of Chinese traditional medicine back then. It also showed just how prepared my mother was to embrace the power of the mind to heal. Her influence rubbed off on me because I embraced belief and its power to transform an insurmountable position into a successful outcome.

Going back to work, albeit two days a week, was my way of getting back to normal; of occupying my mind with something other than thoughts about my treatment or whether the cancer would return. I have never made sickness part of my identity and I didn't intend to start with a cancer diagnosis, but I have to say chemo tested me, particularly when all I felt like doing on Days 13 and 14 was stay in bed. Instead, I got up and researched and wrote tenders, edited newsletters and strategized.

I was starting to get this mind over matter thing, and the very real need to cultivate happiness, despite the pain and despite the sickness of treatment. I was finding happiness in the small things, which were huge milestones for me. I was supremely happy when the cramping stopped on Day 15 of chemo, and I could feel just a little like my pre-cancer self. I was overjoyed when the muscle burn from the incision abated and I could go for a few hours forgetting I had my abdominal muscles cut in two, and a deep purple river of scar tissue down my midline which was still healing months after surgery.

I was happy to sit and look at the blossoms outside my lounge-room window or when my youngest son walked through the door, with his face full of youthful consideration and expectation. I was happy to sit with my husband in quiet companionship. I was sublimely happy on my daily walks with my dogs; to see the green fields and blue skies and feel the breeze on my face, and the warmth on my bare arms. I felt lucky and grateful that I survived cancer, and it filled me with an exuberant yet simple joy in living.

When I went out to lunch or for a cup of tea with friends, I took more notice of the people around me. I learnt to pick those who were burdened by life because that was the way I'd been before cancer. They were the people who rarely noticed other people, so consumed by their own thoughts and never knowing how lucky they were to be alive.

I had never understood the term "living in a state of grace" before, but I think that cancer made me understand that. Grace was the deep well of gratitude I felt for being alive and finding the simple joy in living.

Cancer was also teaching me to be discerning. As my treatment progressed through the prescribed chemo rounds, and with the big-ticket item (my operation) out of the way, I began to think seriously about the future. How did I want to live, who did I want to share this precious life with? And more to the point, who and what did I need to let go of?

I began to think about those situations in my life that were clearly dysfunctional; that had been dysfunctional over several years, some over a lifetime. I knew that I would only get one chance at living this life and I wasn't prepared to waste too much time anymore. I began to set boundaries in personal relationships that previously I had allowed way too much latitude. I took a leaf out of my mum's book and steeled my mind against those situations that made my heart ache, and my mind race with "what if" thoughts. I began to take steps to stay well, and I began to become quite determined about seeing it through, regardless of what some people might think.

I knew that, ultimately, I had the right to make those decisions. The diagnosis of cancer had shown me that I had the right to happiness and the right to jettison dysfunction that made me unhappy.

Certainly, during treatment, when I needed every advantage, it was in my interest to use my mind to cultivate happiness.

As Round Two of chemo loomed and I contemplated whether the horrendous nausea and stomach cramps would reappear, I pushed aside the things that normally would dim my spirit. Instead, I focused on what gave me joy, not what took it away.

Chapter 13

Keeping On, Keeping On...

Honesty is the first chapter in the book of wisdom.
Thomas Jefferson

Round Two of chemo came and went and so did the nausea, fatigue and a new side effect, sore feet. Symptoms were cumulative and worse in the second week, and particularly the last few days. A check up with my oncologist confirmed I could stay on six chemo tablets a day rather than go up to eight.

"Oh my God, I can hardly handle six let alone adding another two," I protested.

"No, no, we'll keep you on six (500mg) a day," he said.

I sighed with relief and made a mental note to stop trying to tell my oncologist what to do. He was a quiet and respectful man, but I'm sure patients like me, who are fully informed about treatment make his job more challenging. But I was hugely thankful he didn't up my dose as I was barely hanging on in that last week, without risking more ill health.

My blood tests revealed several side effects from chemo were starting to tell on my body, high phosphorous and low lymphocytes, which are a subset of white blood cell counts, had my pathologist suggesting I be investigated for Lymphopenia.

"It should clear once the chemo is finished," my oncologist said. "It is not something we worry about too much. We worry more about neutrophils rather than lymphocytes."

Okay for you to say that, I thought to myself. I worried about permanent effects from chemotherapy, but what could I do? I was committed to the course. I had to go through it, to get beyond it. I didn't care that the statistics revealed chemo provided such a small percentage of coverage. I wanted to make use of that extra 5% chance at protecting against recurrence. I felt I'd fought so hard, all year, that not having chemo would be a mistake, a bit like giving in before the fight was finished.

At the end of Round Two I was thankful I was handling the chemo albeit with side effects that I was able to manage. The night before I finished the round, I began thinking of all my friends that didn't know I had cancer and I realized they had a right to know. In fact, now the major operation was over, I wanted to "come out of the closet" so to speak. I wanted to talk openly about my experiences and let people know what I'd been through, how it had changed me for the better and to warn them to get checked out if they had any symptoms which may or may not be cancer. So, I wrote a blog and posted it on Facebook.

At the beginning of this year, I was diagnosed with colon cancer.

It sent me into shock for months and I told very few people. I wanted privacy and time to deal with my own emotions rather than worrying about what other people were feeling. The other reason for privacy was fear of my looming major surgery.

I was right to be fearful. It was a huge and dreadful surgery that my surgeon likened to open heart surgery in its invasive-ness. What a relief I felt when it was over, even though the road to rehabilitation was long and hard with a post-operative wound infection and other complications.

For the first time in my life, I experienced total and utter physical helplessness. I could hardly move, except to go from the bed to the chair. The pain levels were acute, and I have a reasonably high pain threshold.

It was a good milestone to get out of the road. Then as soon as I was feeling a little bit better, it was time to get back on the chemotherapy treadmill (I had 5.5 weeks of radiation and chemo in March/April).

Cancer teaches you many things. It has been the single, most defining moment in my life — aside from bringing children into this world. It has changed me beyond what I thought would be possible. It has changed me for the better.

That's shocked you, hasn't it. How could getting cancer change you for the better? It's hard to explain but I'll try because it's hard to understand for people who have lived without a serious disease or illness that could take their lives.

The easiest way to describe it is that I no longer live my life on some sort of invisible autopilot. I now make the most of each day and I am joyful to see a sunrise. I take great pleasure in the smallest things, in living a simple life — in a sunny day dotted with yellow daisies and brilliant green earth and trees that are responding to the spring, right before my eyes.

I have a heightened sense of awareness now, perhaps because I live in the moment; in the now.

I have a strengthened belief in God or Buddha or the divine presence ... whatever it is that you want to call divinity. Names don't matter much really.

It sounds cliched but I see the sheer power of love to change everything in the universe. At the end of the day, it is all that matters.

If something or someone bothers me now, I simply turn away. Time is precious and I don't want to waste it on people or situations that are not doing me any good. I value happiness and that simple joy I feel most days.

That ability to decide and act in my own best interests has finally lifted my self-esteem which has been a lifelong struggle. It feels good to be free.

I was lucky. I had early-stage cancer and for most people, if it is caught early, it is curable. I hope I'm cured.

So tonight, I finished Round Two of chemo. That's two down and four to go. I'm whittling it away and looking forward to the day when I don't have to poison my body anymore and cope with the resultant side effects.

I would urge anyone with any symptoms no matter how slight, to get them checked out. Don't ignore what your body might be trying to tell you.

Yes, the worst can happen in life but it's entirely possible to recover and emerge stronger and better than before.

Namaste.

The blog was well received. One friend said it was like I "was giving a gift to my friends through sharing my cancer journey." My blog had the highest number of hits that day. I knew then that I had to continue to write about my fight with colon cancer because every person who reads about my experiences might think twice before ignoring symptoms.

Chapter 14

Love Is ... Caring

Love is the ability and willingness to allow
those that you care for to be what they choose
for themselves without any insistence that they
satisfy you.

Wayne Dyer

I have been both cancer carer and cancer fighter and I know
that the carer's road is a tough one too. When your loved one
is fighting cancer, they are undergoing deep changes that you
may not understand — like I said at the beginning of this book,
cancer changes you and, hopefully, makes you a better and
stronger person. However, it's not easy to see a loved one change
before your eyes; become more independent and, sometimes,
more forceful.

One of the ways I changed was in finding my voice. I'd
been largely introverted before cancer and, yes, shy. Sure,
I got better at hiding this over the years and, outwardly,
appeared confident. Inwardly, I often felt small and would
suppress my voice just to keep life running smoothly, or
what I thought was smoothly. Cancer opened me up to the
possibility that it is not a bad thing to let people know how
you feel or what you want. In fact, people respect the honesty
and the boundaries you set.

As one of the carers for my sister I also understand what it's
like to witness changes in your loved one, when they are under
the pressure, pain and suffering cancer brings.

I recall when I first came home from hospital. As soon as I
hobbled in the door, I wanted to do the housework. Of course,
it had already been done and I was in too much pain to achieve

anything around the house then, and for a very long time. I had significant pain in my incision site and no matter how many loose pants I tried on, I couldn't find one that didn't add to the pain. My sisters managed to find at least eight pairs for me, but none were any good. It was a frustrating and painful time for me. But that is what being a carer is all about, anticipating needs, stepping back when required and persisting with love despite the changes your loved one might be facing, whether that is through decreased mobility in the short term, or changes in their body image such as scarring.

My husband was my main carer throughout my illness and did a brilliant job though I could see times when he was frustrated with a particular request of mine: when he was tired too and I asked him to do something for me because I was sick from the chemo or experiencing the ongoing muscle burn at the incision site. In many ways he was also my coach, urging me toward physical activity, telling me not to "stoop," advising me when I might be doing something that was not in my long-term interests.

He wasn't overbearing with his advice, just sensible and constant. For me, this is the definition of support: constant, gentle but firm advice and action. His unwavering support through my cancer journey was a touchstone in our long relationship. Like my husband, my children reacted to my cancer by rallying and providing watchful and considerate support.

I am forever grateful to those who supported and cared for me; to my sisters who cared for me after my operation. To my brothers and my nieces and nephews with their constant source of texts, always wishing me well, and to my wonderful network of friends who came through with solid and unwavering support; I couldn't have gone through this journey alone.

Caring for a loved one facing the long and grueling treatment that colon cancer brings, is not easy. It is natural to think that after the major operation — the colon resection — that caring is finished. It isn't. Just like everything else, the end of the race might be in sight but there are still the hardest miles to run.

Cancer treatment does not leave you unscathed. There are the incision sites, sometimes incisional hernias to be fixed, there is the loss of muscles, nerves and physical fitness, as well as the loss of independence.

My strongest advice is for carers to have patience when a loved one may be acting out of character — perhaps it's their fear, or the pain, talking. Step back, be patient and things will right themselves. Remember your loved one is in the fight of their life. You just need to have their back while they fight.

And my fight, at this point, was far from over. I still had chemo to finish and another operation to face.

Chapter 15

Hardest Part of the Climb

Even rats can only be kicked around for so long
before they've had enough.

Joe Cowley

I parked the car and got out slowly. I was dragging my feet into
the oncology unit yet again. Round Three and I could barely
lift my mood above cynical at best. The truth was I was tired —
tired from the chemo, tired from the cancer fight and tired
of wondering how long I would stay No Evidence of Disease
(NED). A young couple got out of a small car, parked next to
me. He held her hand; she looked a little fearful. I assumed she
was undergoing cancer treatment too. I smiled and reminded
myself that there were others doing it tough — perhaps tougher
than me. I had a good prognosis while others may not.

I quickened my pace; best get this bloody thing over and
done with. They were nice, the nurses, asking me how I was
going, suggesting stronger anti-nausea meds and telling me
that, unfortunately, fatigue went hand in hand with chemo. I
showed them the tiny pustules that had broken out on one arm.

"Go and see your GP if they get worse. Don't try and manage
on your own," the nurse told me, handing me my two-week
supply of cytotoxic poison.

"Yes, I will," I replied, knowing full well I wouldn't go unless
I was covered in them. I'd had enough of doctors and enough of
cancer treatment. Well, at least that's how I felt that morning.

I asked for a copy of my blood tests. The usual things
were outside of normal range. Lymphocytes low — query
lymphopenia the pathologist suggested. Liver function tests a

bit skewed and something else: slight cytotoxicity found in red blood cells.

Great. That's what I was murmuring to myself all the way home and through breakfast as I popped the poison. It's no wonder chemo was such a bumpy road. They take you as close to the edge with side effects as you can. When you get too sick, they'll reduce the dosage but until that point, put up and shut up.

I was in no mood for the day ahead, so I decided to go easy on myself. I would do my morning's work for my boss but once I'd clocked off, well, the afternoon would be a lazy one. I had to find some way of making myself feel better of jolting myself out of my world-weary, cynical mood. I knew it would get me nowhere.

That's the thing about having had cancer, you know that no matter how bad things get, you have to deal with them because if you don't, they'll deal with you. Unhappiness is not good for your health. It's a waste of time, but I wasn't ready to bounce back and tango round the kitchen. It had been a long, hard, hard year and chemo was the poisonous icing on the cake. So, I took the afternoon off. I read and I allowed myself to reason that I was almost halfway through chemo. I went onto my online support group site and read the thread about cancer being the easiest to cure if it is caught reasonably early. I nodded at the comment: "Colon cancer treatment certainly ages you." I thought of myself slowly taking the stairs at night with chemo-laden legs. I climbed into bed early for a change and let the tiredness come. Tomorrow would be another day and I was lucky to be alive. The last vestiges of cynicism drifted away with sleep.

***

Most people go overseas for their big midlife break whereas I got to fight cancer for a year. That was the tag line echoing in my mind as Round Four of chemo loomed and I made my way, again, to the oncology department to pick up the dreaded little pink poisonous pills. Round Three had been a tough one for some reason. Insomnia had set in which I understand is a side effect of Capecitabine and I had had successive nights with as little as three to four hours of sleep. I would get up around 1.00 a.m. and then again around 3.00 a.m., and then again around 5.30 a.m. That was an average night's sleep unfortunately and, as I couldn't manage to go to sleep before 11.00 p.m., I was getting hardly more than two hours sleep straight before I woke. This meant that the fatigue caused by Capecitabine was so much worse, particularly in the second week of the cycle.

The little pustules on my arms persisted through to Round Four, with some ulcers in the mouth and, on my most fatigued day, heart palpitations. By the end of Round Three, I had decided I was doing too much and became resentful of impositions. I made the decision to do Round Four more easily by cutting right back on social engagements and resting on my non-workdays. Instead of conquering the weekly spring clean, I paid my son to do the floors, who was eager for pocket money anyway. Wherever I could see a shortcut, I took it.

About halfway through Round Three, I hit a huge downer. It was brought on by the death of a cancer fighter — a gracious, beautiful lady that I had friended on Facebook and kept up a consistent communication with through inboxing. She was a strong fighter but unfortunately the aggressiveness of her cancer which had metastasized to the liver, won in the end. She passed suddenly and unexpectedly, and it was enough to send me into a spin. It coincided with huge chunks of my hair falling out. I wrote a very depressing blog titled *Cumulus Greyous*. Of course, I made light of what was real depression looming. It was the old black dog that I'd fought periodically throughout my life; that despairing feeling that nothing would be any good. The feeling of hopelessness; why fight this horrible disease? Would it come back? There were no guarantees in life, and, at any moment, it could all be taken away as it had with my friend.

A few of my close friends responded and I met them on the weekend for "tea and sympathy." We spent hours in cafes just talking about cancer. I was lucky in that my friends had battled cancer and knew what I was going through. Looking back to Round Three, fatigue played a part in my low mood. When you are exhausted, with the kind of exhaustion chemo brings, it is hard to stay ready and willing in the trenches. With a great deal of determination on the week off between rounds, I got back to my "happy place" and began anticipating the future again. I consulted the calendar and soaked up the fact that my chemo would finish on 12 January 2016 — in just two months. Already I was more than halfway through it.

I found if I rested and controlled the fatigue, then my mood improved. I've always tried to be positively oriented, and this has worked well for me, particularly when I managed to control my depression. My mum used to say, "When you are up, you are up and when you are down, you are down. You've just got to roll with the punches." But try as I might, I never learnt to "roll with the punches," and that was the way it was when this beautiful lady passed unexpectedly.

So, as I walked into oncology, I was disciplined. I had a game plan; I had grieved for my friend, and I was better managing my fatigue. I had psyched myself up for Round Four, concentrating on the positives. I was a good fighter again, well prepared to go the distance to the final round.

Round Four had been difficult. The fatigue had increased, and I was taking sleeping tablets at night. It had been almost six months since the surgery and I was getting tired of the constant weariness, of pushing my body to heal and of trying to stay on top of the chemo.

I missed my mum who passed away in 2010 and thought bitterly about my diagnosis almost 12 months prior. By the time

I finished complete treatment, it would be around two years. That's a long time to be mentally strong and positive.

"I've tried so hard to be positive," I cried over the phone to my sister. "I've done everything I could. Now I don't care anymore."

My sister was sympathetic. "I think you get to a point where your body has had enough."

I nodded. I had. The radiation had been brutal, the operation had destroyed my core strength and left me almost in daily pain. The chemo had given me insomnia and fatigue and I'd lost strength on my right side. It was five months since the operation, yet I was still on painkillers at night for the muscle burn. I didn't have half the stamina I used to, and I felt old before my time. Life was not fair and, despite my usual ability to bounce back, I didn't. Perhaps it was the thought that I had two more rounds of chemo to complete, and another operation to get through, or maybe I was just asking why me?

I took a little comfort in my sister's sympathy and kind words but really, I just wanted to be by myself. I remembered a poem I'd written for my mum when I was about 11 years old. It was about the loss of innocence. I'd lost my drive to work hard to get back to normal. It was just all too hard.

So, I took some time off. I walked less and canceled social engagements. I felt like I'd had a shock to the system, and I wanted to go within, center myself and re-find my strength. Only then would I regain my drive and positivity; the two things that had meant I was still working through treatment, exercising daily, strategizing the best pathways through treatment and handling the side effects of chemotherapy reasonably well.

"I'm tired," I had told my surgeon at my next visit.

"You just want to be cured," he said.

"Yes, I do."

It was with reduced willpower I walked into Round Five; the only bright spot on the horizon was it was the second to last round of chemo. I needed to find acceptance again, and I needed to learn patience. Most of all I needed to reconnect with faith and hope; the two beliefs that led to positivity.

Taking a bit of time out and slowing down, I hoped to rediscover the positivity that had guided my healing so far.

And so, I did. Each round was totally different and Round Five proved no exception. It began with an extremely positive meeting with my oncologist who, incidentally, wore the most gorgeous pair of orange and blue sandals I'd ever seen.

"I really like your shoes," I remarked.

He smiled. "How are you?"

"Good, good. I can't complain. It's all doable," I finished, confidently.

He responded immediately. "You look well."

"Thanks. I feel okay. A bit of nausea and fatigue, and I'm on sleeping tablets now for the insomnia."

He gave me some good advice about not taking the tablets on the week off chemo because it made them more effective and ordered some more blood tests and testing of the cancer markers, my CEA which measures colon cancer in the body and 19-9 which measures other cancers such as pancreatic. My biggest win was that I didn't need to have a CT scan until May of the next year.

"Yay no scanxiety for Christmas," I said, very pleased with the way the meeting was going.

He finished the appointment by rescheduling me for May.

"I don't have to see you before then because you're doing so well, I think you'll finish chemo on time on 12 January."

That was just over a month away. I couldn't believe it. I thanked him and left with a spring in my step. Yeah, sure I'd had a lot of nausea that day and I hadn't slept well but nothing could dent my spirits — I was on track to finish chemo which, in a way, except for my reversal, was the last of my treatment.

Walking out into the sunshine of the day, I was full of gratitude that my chemo treatment was coming to an end, so unlike just a week before when I was struggling with side effects, but it is the dark and the struggles which help us appreciate the light.

Chapter 16

The Best of News

The happiest of endings begin with a struggle so embrace yours.

Nomzamo Nhlumayo

Good news. The best of news. I was ready for it. I'd managed to get through chemo, radiation, surgery, and more chemo. One final reconstructive surgery remained. Like all cancer warriors, I'd worked hard. I just wanted the treatment to be finished. I turned on my computer, ready for another day of writing and interacting through my work. It was going to be a busy day. That was good. I was ready for it. I was happy. Happy because a little voice of optimism was telling me that, just possibly, I would be okay.

Honestly? Between the invasive tests and treatment, my body had been irrevocably changed. Treatment is grueling and its effects linger long after it finishes.

I remember sitting in an easy chair not daring to move too much after my surgery for fear of disturbing a long abdominal incision. I had put the pathology results away to read when I got home from hospital and, as I sat immobile in the chair, I knew I could not put it off any longer — for better or worse, pathology tells you a lot about your survivability from cancer.

My surgeon had preconditioned me in hospital saying, "I think you will be pleased with the pathology results." And I was. Margins clear, cancer had not broken through the colon wall, not in the blood supply and not in lymph nodes. It was nowhere else in my body. The chemo/radiation they'd given me before my operation had shrunk the tumor and I was downstaged via the pathology to stage one. That was a pretty good result and worth the pain and suffering that I'd undergone as part of treatment.

As I grappled with Round Five of Six in the mop-up chemo cycle — my insurance policy — I thought of the cost of treatment, physically and mentally. When I looked back on the fitness I had before the surgery and now, there's no comparison. I'd healed well, and I'm very grateful for that, but the reality was that my body had been altered forever. Then there were the ongoing side effects from radiation and chemotherapy. Pelvic radiation, particularly, was very brutal for me. Unfortunately, the treatment for cancer is invasive but critical if you want to stay alive; if I had not undergone my treatment, I'd be dead in a couple of years.

That is the reality; you live with the side effects for the rest of your, hopefully, long life. Cancer is life-threatening and treatment can and does kill people. It's why when people finish their treatment, they often have the psychological breakdown they could have had in the middle of treatment but didn't because all they thought about was powering towards survival.

Sometimes I catch a glimpse of all that I've been through, and it throws me. Most of the time I'm positively happy that I got a second chance in this lifetime.

So, what was I going to do with that second chance? I realized that the universe had a purpose for me, and that like the faith that sustained me through treatment, that it would become clear in its own time. And it did.

One of my strongest goals was to get fit and ready physically and mentally for that purpose. I was healing and beginning to see that, perhaps, my purpose was to be a healer, drawing on my experiences with a life-threatening disease. The seed was planted.

Chapter 17

Ho, Ho, Ho

Don't let the past steal your present. This is the message of Christmas: We are never alone.

Taylor Caldwell

There is something reverent about Christmas and the end of the year. It's a sacred time, where memories of the past come flooding back and we get to really think about the events and the people that are important to us. The end of 2015 gave me plenty to mull over. I approached this with a sense of gratitude and acknowledgment of just how lucky I'd been to catch my cancer early.

While I've been better at looking after my health at different times in my life than others, I wasn't doing all I could for my health at the time of my diagnosis. I let other people's problems weigh on me and I took burdens and responsibilities when they weren't mine to carry. As an empath it was hard not to — I sense the undercurrents and they worry me, whereas a "normal" person would not give someone's mood another thought. They certainly wouldn't feel responsible for it, which is how I had been in the past. Let me give you an example: if someone is putting on a brave face but inwardly angry, worried, or sad, I know it when they enter a room, without them saying anything, and I try and fix it. You can't "fix" other people, nor take responsibility for them, but I used to try. Now I acknowledge that it is their path and that I have enough of my own worries to try and "fix." I'm much more willing to see that I (like everyone else) am a precious human soul that needs nurturing, loving, and looking after. Self-love was one of the biggest gifts of cancer.

Like most others, before cancer I enjoyed a social life — a drink and good food, but too much of a good thing is never a good thing. Now I'm less inclined to give into weakness and I practice moderation in all things. A life of limitation is only as limiting as you make it. Now, I replace vice with victory and rarely overindulge. It's the discipline that comes with age, and experience. That's not to say that I don't allow myself the occasional treat, I do — and guess what — it tastes and feels twice as good.

And then there was exercise. While I've pounded the pavement and swum for miles every day, I was never consistent with it, year in year out. Rather I exercised in bursts. Now I walk or ride my bike daily and one of my best Christmas presents was an electronic bracelet which measures the kilometers I've walked each day. I am now walking at least three to four kilometers a day — this activity from a couch potato who upon remembering the competitive sports of youth, hit the gym or pool hard, for all of a couple of months of the year.

However, one of the biggest reflections for me that Christmas brought was on gratitude. I experienced and felt everything more keenly. I may have had to pop the dreaded chemo pills over Christmas but that didn't stop me trying to give as much as I could to my family. I did this because I knew that had my diagnosis been different, I may have been absent for this Christmas, or struggling to survive.

I cooked *the* most beautiful turkey, stuffed with a ham, onion, herb and garlic mixture and I basted a huge ham with the best glaze that I've used year after year because it is so divine. My husband and I shopped up a storm, buying trolley-loads of treats, individual Christmas puddings, strudels and Panettone, a wonderful European invention.

I allowed myself a couple of glasses of wine which I sipped slowly through dinner and the hilarious card games which followed. I had a good Christmas, despite the chemo.

But behind positivity there was also a sense of the magnitude of what I experienced in 2015. I tried not to look too hard or think too long. There was the awful radiation and chemo, the huge six-hour operation and the mop-up chemo when your body has had enough. As always, I returned to that feeling of gratitude; that cancer is commonplace, and I had faced it and survived to this point, and that my prognosis was good. I thought of how much I'd grown spiritually because of cancer; that I'd felt invisibly supported by something greater than what we can realize here on earth. It reflected in all the signs that had been placed in my path to testify that "yes, you are going to be okay; you are going to survive this."

That's what I thought over Christmas and as we rang in the New Year. I also thought about something higher than myself. I was very lucky to be able to use my cancer experiences to grow spiritually. Cancer had not silenced me; on the contrary, it had given me my voice.

As 2015 ticked over to 2016, I wondered what purpose I had yet to fulfill. I didn't have any answers, but I did know for sure that the right things happen at the right time.

That Christmas I looked forward, not backwards. I decided to continue my tertiary study — because the uni that I kept asking for deferrals from said, "study this semester or lose your place," and I wanted to somehow try and work with people that had been through life-changing experiences.

My chemo finished on 12 January and one of my biggest milestones loomed: the last surgery.

As it turned out, the surgery was easy in comparison to my major surgery, far less complicated. One and a half hours in theater compared to six and a half hours for my major surgery. With chemo finished, and good pathology results, it was time to get on with my life.

Chapter 18

I Should Be Happy…

When you come out of the storm, you won't be the same person who walked in. That's what this storm's all about.

Haruki Murakami, *Kafka on the Shore*

The lull between treatment, finishing six rounds of chemo and waiting for the final surgery brought an unexpected and unwanted sense of abandonment and confusion. I believed this new and equally difficult part of my journey was brought on because I had time to think about what had happened to me in the preceding year. I had been fighting the cancer with everything I had and when there was no fighting needed for a time, I had time to think. My first thought was, "what just happened to me?" I began to think about the risk the cancer might return and that I'd had a series of disasters since 2010 with my mum's passing. At the end of 2013, my sister's own cancer diagnosis and, in 2014, the suicide of my friend, followed by my own battle with cancer in 2015. It was too much darkness, too many shocks and I gave into the terrible sense of fear, aloneness and anxiety that had been lurking at the back of my spirit for some months. I was overwhelmed and my usual coping mechanisms were failing me. I felt different from everybody else; that I had knowledge they didn't, but it was a horrible, negatively oriented knowledge I couldn't shake off. It was the knowledge that while you toil away in life building your dreams, working hard each day, raising a family, and driving yourself forward, it was pointless because it can all be taken away with a cancer diagnosis. While you think you have a purpose, you might not. Happy endings might be a myth. You strived for a lifetime only to die at the end of all that hard work and, if you're unlucky, sooner. Oh, for the sweet bliss of ignorance and denial.

I had lost my compass and my world view, and I had been shaken to the core. I felt like I was spinning out of control and off my axis. I responded by shutting myself off from the world and going through the motions each day. I desperately wanted a new start in life, but I didn't know where to begin. I only knew that to live in the same way as before was unacceptable. I waited for a guru to appear, but no one showed up. I ground to a halt, stuck in gray days and somber tones.

My motivation was gone.

If there was any chance of salvaging my motivation for life, it disappeared when my elder sister told me the colon cancer had metastasized in her liver. That was the final shock that pushed me towards seeing a therapist. I had seen a counselor in 2013 when I was going through a difficult phase, and she had restored my optimism, confidence, and belief in myself. I couldn't wait for the appointment because at times I could barely breathe through the feeling of being utterly overwhelmed by death and darkness. It was a desperate feeling, this loss of a steady compass that all would be well.

I told her my story, not pausing while taking her through the events since 2013 and finishing with the latest blow, that my sister now had stage 4 colon cancer. My therapist was non-judgmental, patient and, as usual, able to nail my problems.

"If I could say a few words to you that you might like to consider, they would be 'fear and worry.' You have had multiple shocks, and you are feeling overwhelmed by fear."

She went on to say that fear will always take you to the future and that I was overthinking, and that my thoughts were predominantly fearful.

"You have to live in the present moment, bring yourself back into your body and concentrate on the present. What you're feeling is perfectly natural. You've had not one but several shocks and anyone who experienced the same would be reacting in the same way."

I confessed I had no motivation for my work, or for my current lifestyle. I told her that while I should be rejoicing in every new day and being cancer free, I was instead "just going through the motions."

"We are all living like we have all the time in the world when we don't. Everything, all the striving in life, seems pointless," I said.

"You are depressed. I would like you to ask your GP about anti-depressants — just to tie you over, give you some breathing space," she said.

I wasn't so sure about anti-depressants. I hadn't taken them before, and I didn't want to start. I told her I would think about it but start using the tools she'd given me to manage the fear and worry. I acknowledged that maybe I had gone back to work too soon, that I hadn't given myself the time and the space to process what had happened to me. I had been so keen to normalise my life which is what every cancer fighter wants; to go back to their normal life.

We arranged another appointment. Driving home, I mulled over her words and admitted that fear and anxiety were throwing a pall over my life. As I had been leaving, she had reassured me that I would feel normal again one day.

"You are not yourself now. I know you don't want to hear this, but you will feel normal again and you will put your life back together."

Within three days I was at the Emergency Department with an acute bladder infection, its severity caused, in part, by the radiation damage to my bladder in 2015. Radiation, although lowering my chances of the cancer coming back at the site, also appeared to be the "gift that keeps giving." It had burnt and damaged my pelvis and, particularly, my bladder.

As I lay hooked up to IV antibiotics, I wondered if life would ever return to normal again. I find that people who have not tasted the insidious, life shattering impacts of cancer, do not understand the reality changes that cancer victims and survivors experience.

And cancer is commonplace. I was to learn again that night just how commonplace. The night sister who was assigned to my care reminded me.

"My husband also had colon cancer, early stage, like you," she said. "Five years later, it's come back in his liver."

"Oh no," I said, genuinely upset at her news.

Her eyes filled with tears. "It's inoperable. Right through his liver."

"I'm so sorry," I said, not really knowing what else to say.

When she left to do her rounds, her words stayed with me. Was there no end to the devastation that cancer brought to families?

I didn't sleep much that night but the next morning I felt much better physically. The pain had subsided dramatically with the IV antibiotics, and I was able to enjoy the omelette they brought for breakfast. I was eating that and sipping my cup of tea, feeling pleased that I would most likely go home that morning, when I heard a voice from across the corridor.

"Hello, Maryann."

I didn't have my glasses on and couldn't make out the face.

"Who is that?"

"It's Dale," she said.

"Oh hi," I replied. I had seen a woman brought in the night before by ambulance and I knew she wasn't well but didn't know it was my old work mate Dale. "What's wrong?"

She waved her hand across her body. "The cancer has come back. It's everywhere."

For the second time in less than 24 hours, I didn't know what to say. Years earlier I had worked with this lovely lady who had been diagnosed with breast cancer but after treatment went on to live a normal life.

"I'm so sorry. I was diagnosed with colon cancer in 2015. What do you do?"

She smiled. "Not much you can do. I'm just taking it one day at a time."

When my husband came to pick me up, I made sure we stopped by Dale's bedside to wish her well.

As I walked out of the hospital door, I reflected that not only had the severity of my cancer treatment come back to haunt me, but I had also seen, yet again, there were no guarantees with cancer.

As I rested over the weekend, I felt a new sense of calm. I thought about how hard I'd tried to return to normal and that it was time to admit that I was changed forever by cancer. I wasn't as strong physically and my mental and emotional outlook had changed. It was time to admit to myself that my life would be forever changed by cancer and there was no going back to normal.

What did the future hold? I didn't know. Would the cancer come back? I didn't know that either. How would I live my life going forward? I hadn't a clue. All I had was each day, step by step, as best I could. After a year of cancer treatment, it was finally a relief to let go of the myth of normality which, instinctively, didn't ring true to me anymore.

However, a small voice inside still whispered hope. I began to think about the possibility of using my experiences in my work. I also thought about getting off the treadmill of a "career" occupying my goal setting for the future. I knew I wanted to live more spiritually, keeping my body healthy and my mind and emotions stress free. I knew there would be changes to come; that I had a different destination to get to and one that fully acknowledged my journey with cancer and a deep-felt acknowledgement that it had irrevocably changed me. Anything in my post-cancer life journey that didn't reflect my new reality, not defined by cancer but changed by cancer, was just window dressing and marking time.

I was moving into the "survivorship" stage. I knew that. What I didn't know was how to navigate this new stage. I began reading about it and realized the medical profession and organizations like the Cancer Council in Australia were also acknowledging the difficulties of getting back to normal after cancer diagnosis and treatment. There was acknowledgement of the "collateral damage" cancer treatment can cause, and of the mental and emotional anguish it wreaks. These side effects are not easily, simply or quickly solved. Survivorship is often hard, and there is also a sense of guilt as well for those who don't survive or have a poorer prognosis.

When I was diagnosed in January 2015, my friend and her husband visited unexpectedly. My friend wanted to see me but also to let me know that her husband had been diagnosed with pancreatic cancer. As I fought my battle, he fought his only to see his cancer spread to the lungs and eventually take his life.

Whenever I heard bad news like this, and including the nurse's husband's inoperable liver secondaries, I felt a mixture of emotions from relief I was still cancer free, through to increased fear my cancer might recur and a feeling of guilt that my prognosis was good. Of course, I knew this was not entirely rational or logical, but it didn't stop the emotional responses.

Survivorship was turning out to be less manageable than I had originally thought. I used to wish for the end of treatment and returning to normal. It was a shock to tick off the boxes of treatment milestones, only to descend into an emotional mess.

I didn't have any answers, and like at the beginning of my cancer treatment, I had to rely on my faith, and hope that everything would be okay when I had absolutely no guarantees.

Chapter 19

Not the Same ... Different

Freedom is an internal achievement rather than an external adjustment.

Powell Clayton

If someone had told me at the time of diagnosis that my life would never return to normal again, that I would live with cancer as a strange life partner for a long time after treatment finished, and that I would learn what it truly means to be physically *dis*-abled, I wonder if I would have fought so bravely and, well, naively.

I fought with the expectation of returning to normal life — you get sick, you recover, you move on. That's not the way it works with cancer, though, if you're lucky enough to survive it. Cancer picked me up like a tornado and left me far from the place I knew as normal, and when I finally made it home, it was a place I didn't know.

So many aspects of my life had changed since January 2015. I no longer took anything for granted. Almost three years from that fateful day I had my colonoscopy in Five Dock, Sydney, I was in remission, but I also had to learn to live with the reality that cancer can return any time. They ran surveillance testing on me for the first five years. When I made it past that time limit cancer free, then I was considered cured but with every three-monthly blood test the old fears and anxieties return.

How do you learn to live with the constancy of the "it might come back" thought, particularly with the constant testing? It's not easy, but you adjust. You don't make long-term plans, you set short-term goals, and you subconsciously start to plan to do the things you've always wanted to do. You live more in the moment; you learn to live as freely as you can. You don't waste time and you don't tolerate fools. You are more compassionate as you've felt real pain and suffering. You understand another's suffering only too well. You reassess and you start to think: why am I here?

Despite the tornado and the displacement of cancer treatment, and post-cancer life, my spirituality was still solid. I understood that I was still here because there is much to learn and much to give back. I am still finding my way and, at times, particularly, my belief in myself. Major transitions take time. Healing takes time. I've only just started on my quest.

One of the biggest adjustments was the acceptance that it is no longer possible to work as I used to, hard, long hours, and away from home. For someone who built an identity on a career, it was a tough adjustment. The impacts of radiation and chemo, and major surgery, have meant that the long, consecutive days I used to do before cancer are no longer possible. But I have limited motivation to return to my old career anyway. It's a question I ask myself: why go through your cancer journey only to return to my same lifestyle?

Everything has changed; I've lost parts of myself, gained new understandings, and found hidden strengths built on resilience only those who've experienced cancer or major life setbacks, can understand.

I've experienced pain and suffering, and I've witnessed the strength that faith, belief, and hope can deliver during adversity. Cancer has delivered seismic shocks through my life and, at times, left me wrecked and bereft but they have also moved old patterns and self-limiting beliefs. I don't live my life in the same way as I did before cancer. Not even close.

As soon as I could, I resumed my university studies with the aim of finishing my Bachelor of Social Sciences (Social Welfare). I graduated in 2018. I've also became interested in some of the techniques I used throughout my treatment — visualization, meditation, and energy healing. I enrolled in Reiki I and Reiki II and practiced on myself. Combined with meditation, Reiki had a beneficial impact on my digestive system, calming and soothing.

Despite being spiritually minded, in many ways I feel my real spiritual journey is just beginning. Like a builder surveying an empty block of land, I am wondering what I will build. As yet, I can't see what the house will look like, but I know that I will belong in it.

I have returned to contract government consultancy and professional writing for as long as my health allows in any one week. It's enough to generate an income, provide some workplace goal setting and increase my social interactions. Cancer can be lonely sometimes.

Some of my friendships have weathered the storm; some haven't. Those that have gone were based on what I could give as a career driven, seemingly strong individual who was larger than life. Now I am quieter, less willing to take control of other people's issues, less inclined to rush to the rescue. I understand that everyone's journey is uniquely their own and that only they are responsible for their happiness, as well as their distress.

Every now and then I hear myself laugh, a light-hearted and happy sound. That is part of the old me and I'm glad it's still there. I hope that as more time unfolds, with new situations and opportunities, that I laugh more. I'd be happy with that.

I do know that we must make the most of the present moment. It's the only thing that is guaranteed to any of us.

Chapter 20

Blue Crows

It is said that when a crow comes to you, it brings a message that major change is taking place in your life, and that you can adapt to anything. The crow is a reminder of the creation that resides within us all and in the world around us — the power we have to determine our future.

Unknown

I began writing about my cancer journey around February 2015 after I was diagnosed with colon cancer. I had celebrated my fifty-third birthday a month before I was diagnosed; my youngest son was heading into Year 11 and, as the main breadwinner for the family, I was finally starting to relax a little. There might be a little more freedom round the corner, or so I thought.

Instead, freedom gave way to restriction, potential liberation to a fight for survival. As you have seen from my story, fear was the single biggest emotion that confronted me when I heard those words: "Oh yes, there are definitely cancer cells there..." That fear, along with my old friend's, faith, hope and courage, stayed with me through the long treatment and in its aftermath. In the latter part of my journey something else emerged. It replaced the positiveness and certainty that my life would return to normal. Like a veteran coming to terms with the battlefield, I traveled through post-traumatic stress, depression, and anxiety and finally towards the realization that cancer and its treatment had disabled me, and I would never again return to normal. I was broken and I was weak, physically, mentally, and psychologically.

A long road stretched before me when active treatment finished. Once the daily fight for survival had finished, the drive and determination that is so characteristic of cancer fighters, made way for a listless, new reality. My spiritual compass which had been so strong in the past was shaky with weariness, unable to pinpoint any satisfactory way home.

Where was home? As muted as my mind and emotions were, so too was my spirit. An unrelenting cold wind seemed to blow across the gray landscape that defined my life post-cancer. I began therapy again. I struggled to resume a normal life with the disability that comes when critical bodily parts have been surgically removed, along with the cancerous tumor that invaded them. While no one could see my amputations, they were as real as the war veteran who returned home with missing limbs.

I kept searching for the usual signs from the universe; the hope that my suffering was for a purpose, that old serendipity that had occupied my life before cancer and was responsible for the reprieves and the miraculous during tough times. There were stops and starts, of course — no life is completely devoid of inspiration. I took up Reiki and found an aptitude for hands-on energy work. My psychic senses became more attuned. Despite the spiritual guidance I thought I received, I discovered one sustainable truth: that cancer had opened a gaping wound in my spirit, and it would take discipline and willingness to clean out that wound and heal it. I doubted whether I had the strength to rise like I had done so many times in my life.

Luckily, my spirit — that invisible knowingness — knew which direction to head in, even if my conscious mind and heart was still down that black hole. The first step was to confront my fear, not just to calm myself with Pollyanna thoughts, but to really eliminate the psychological fears, and other negative emotions, that had stunted my growth.

My biggest fear was death.

As a child I was forever rescuing baby lambs left to die by their mothers. Sometimes I was successful. I got to them before the crows managed to swoop and pick their eyes out. From a very young age, I learned to dislike crows despite a deep connection to other birdlife.

When my good friend suicided a year before my cancer diagnosis, I began to be plagued by crows nesting in trees outside my bedroom window. As I dealt with the fallout and grief from his suicide, the crows just wouldn't leave me alone; their endless cawing driving me mad. I spoke to my meditation group about them. "It seems they are trying to tell me something, but I just don't speak crow," I laughed. Their incessant cawing stopped once I was diagnosed but they were still in residence in the trees outside my home.

One day after surgery, radiation and chemo had finished, I was walking on the golf course near my house. The course was unused at specific times of the day, and I was a lone walker with kilometers of beautiful fairways, trees, and landscaped gardens. It was about 4 p.m. on a late winter's afternoon. I was walking up the fairway towards home. At some point I became conscious of a crow flying toward me. What struck me was its color. It wasn't black but a beautiful blue. It flew towards me and then parallel to me, into the afternoon sun. I couldn't take my eyes off it. Rather than the disdain I usually felt for the crows, I was in awe of this one. It was the most beautiful bird I'd ever seen. That moment, which seemed to last forever, began my connection to a bird I'd disliked and perhaps even feared, since my childhood. Rather than the harbinger of death, the black crow became a symbol of life. From that afternoon at least two to three crows accompanied me on my walk. I began to treat them as friends, and I feared less and began to question more.

I like to think those blue crows that first visited me with their incessant cawing, were trying to warn me that cancer was ticking away in my body. I also like to think they are my totem: friends helping me to confront and overcome my fears. It's a long process, rewiring old patterns. There are no magical solutions. There are lessons, though, and I know that because of the blue crows — a symbol of my journey through cancer and beyond, I no longer fear the blackness.

I spoke of change in the introduction to this book. I predicted, quite correctly, when I began writing this book in 2015 that change would dominate my life from cancer diagnosis forward. I thought of change back then as a catalyst — something powerful enough to shift the bedrock of a life. For me, cancer was that change. It brought loss of quality of life, of identity and of physical strength, and "ableness." It delivered loss of my old career and, perhaps most significantly, it was responsible for a loss of innocence; death came out of the closet but so did life.

While cancer simply "train wrecked" a lot of my life, it also changed a lot for the better. I am stronger and more resilient. I understand more; I experience more. I am more. I have knowledge and understanding I never would have had without passing through the furnace of cancer diagnosis and treatment. Spiritually, I have grown in inestimable ways. I rarely ask "why me?"

I also spoke about the need to talk about colon cancer — that it wasn't, and isn't, the "pink" [breast] cancer. In three years of talking to hundreds of colon cancer fighters, I haven't changed my opinion on the urgent need for society to acknowledge that colon cancer is on the rise, and in young people too, and that we need to talk about the symptoms. If there are any changes in colon habits, then speak to your doctor. If he or she doesn't take you seriously, find one who will. Ask for a colonoscopy. Do whatever you have to do to investigate the cause of your symptoms. Don't be put off.

While colon cancer is invasive and treatment harsh, if caught early most colon cancers are treatable. My cancer was caught reasonably early and I'm thankful for that, though never complacent. The point is you don't have to go through what I did. If you are having digestive troubles, please, please get them checked out. At stage 0 or even stage 1, cancerous adenomas may be able to be removed without resection or partial removal of your colon. At this early stage there is also no need for radiation and chemotherapy. You get to dodge a few bullets.

Today, I walk a new path that is transforming my life. I am still on my healing journey with much to learn and experience.

The consistency throughout this book has been the many examples of the presence of a universal life force, guiding and supporting me through intense physical pain and suffering. Nothing about colon cancer and its treatment is easy yet during those long days in hospital, or alone on those gray afternoons with intensifying pain, I always feel the closeness of this life force. It was there in the random coincidences, and it revealed itself through meaning; through white feathers in my path, the friends who called up when needed, and the guides and mentors that "showed up" when most needed.

I know there is no reason to fear the dark, a metaphor for death. My mother often quoted Dylan Thomas's "Do not go gentle into that good night":

Do not go gentle into that good night,
Old age should burn and rave at close of day;
Rage, rage against the dying of the light.

I now understood that we do indeed go on beyond this life into the light of home, not the darkness of oblivion. Knowing that, believing in a spiritual dimension, is mostly enough for me, including on a bad day. My blue crows remind me that I'm never alone — that there is purpose and meaning in this life and that life can be magical, even in the darkest of hours.

How we respond to change does, indeed, determine who we become. Although I am still "becoming," I sometimes get a glimpse of clear blue sky — a look at what my life can be like in the future. I am slowly moving towards that promise, despite the aftermath of cancer and its treatment, and listening to my intuition; understanding that my old life is no longer possible.

As I move through and beyond the colon cancer that altered my life irrevocably, I am beginning to see that this was always my path; the change that provoked a falling away of the old to reveal something new, albeit in its infancy. My journey from here is to nurture and treasure that new life, recognizing that within the blackness there is always the creative potential for life, and light, beyond cancer. My spiritual journey, so entwined with my healing, was only just beginning.

Life is precious.

Meaning, and light, can be found, even in the dark.

Part II

Love, Loss, and Finding a Higher Purpose (2018 – Present Day)

Chapter 21

My Sister Passes

We get no choice. If we love, we grieve.

Thomas Lynch

The most significant thing I must tell you, readers, is about the year my beautiful sister Jane left us. You will have heard her gentle and wise voice throughout these pages. I stopped writing this when she died. For years, I could not revisit the pages here knowing that I had survived, and she didn't, and that I would have to go on without her bright and unfailing friendship and love.

She had always been around — eight years older than me, the "boss" of my brothers and sisters, the mover and shaker, and the one that held us together when our parents died. She was diagnosed in 2013 with the same cancer, in the same place, as mine. I was diagnosed in early 2015 — we navigated cancer together. I helped care for her throughout her treatment, almost like the treatment I received, and then when her cancer metastasized, I was there post-surgeries as a carer. She had an aggressive type of cancer that I didn't, and it unleashed a horrendous battle, only equaled by her courage and willingness to fight it, right to the end. Six years and multiple surgeries, two colon resections, three liver resections and a Whipple surgery. I have never witnessed such willpower and endurance. I doubt I will again, and I never want too again either. What made Jane so different was that her cancer type meant that no chemotherapy worked on her, and so surgery was her only option. She wasn't ready to leave her family, and so she fought hard.

Throughout my treatment she had helped me, as I had helped her. We had helped each other, but then she was gone.

117

It's hard to put into words what it felt like; we had spoken almost daily since her cancer diagnosis in 2013 and weekly, if not twice weekly for most of our lives. We had shared a room while I grew up, I had babysat her children, and worked in her business during my semester breaks, while I was at college. She had been there to look after my children when needed, and she was always my "phone a friend" when the going got tough, and there were plenty of distress calls over the years. However, it was our battle together with the same cancer, in the same place, with virtually the same treatment, that drew us even closer.

When she passed, I could hardly speak to anyone for a long time. From 2010 until her death, I had lost my mum to cancer that year, (and a few years earlier, my dad to cancer), my good friend had taken his own life, I had been diagnosed with cancer, my children had gone through major life events, and finally, my husband had his own battle with cancer. Years later, after studying astrology, I looked back at my transits in 2015. Sure enough, there was Mars (relentless, driven, energy and action) and Pluto (the planet of destruction, transformation, and renewal) in my Eighth House (death and rebirth), a powerful signature that my life would take a 360, and it did.

I have spoken about my clairvoyant ability as a child, misinterpreted as a "vivid imagination" in a Catholic school environment, so very far from the spiritualism I now live by, and the opening of these abilities not only through my cancer battle, but through the absolute end of one "timeline" and the beginning of another. From 2015 I took an immersive deep dive into many healing modalities, studying Reiki and shamanism. I visited healers and studied with them. I knew that my cancer journey was preparing me for my soul's purpose. As I moved further and further away from my mainstream work and lifestyle, and closer to experiencing the joy of spiritual living, I naturally went towards starting my own spiritual platforms on YouTube, Patreon and other social media platforms. *Revealing*

Light: Tarot, Astrology and Spiritualism came into existence in 2018 and has grown exponentially since then to my joy and to my surprise.

One of my biggest cheerleaders at the beginning of my new life post-cancer, was my sister Jane. A farmer's wife, this wasn't her comfort zone, but she encouraged me to keep going in the early days, often standing at the door while I channeled my messages to an early YouTube audience. If any of my extended family and friends were judgmental, she soon set them straight. I was very grateful for her faith in me when everyone else was wondering "what on earth has happened to Maryann?" I guess that is what I miss; however, as my platforms have grown, my own viewers and supporters help to fill that void of support and the validation of purpose and value. Your truest supporters seldom question your value; my sister Jane never underestimated what I was doing spiritually, nor why. I guess she knew me very well.

I am grateful for Jane's faith in me, and for the loyalty of my viewers.

Chapter 22

Healing the Spirit

The world is full of magic things, patiently waiting
for our senses to grow sharper.

W.B. Yeats

I have spent a lot of years studying at universities and with
spiritual mentors and teachers — academic (communications,
writing, political science, education, and social sciences) as well
as spiritual study — shamanism, tarot, astrology, mediumship,
and clairvoyance. It seemed that when I began my spiritual
platforms there was a need to move away from orthodox study
and into the esoteric sciences. I had been using tarot cards most
of my adult life. My first deck, the Aquarian Tarot by the late
David Palladini was purchased in the early 1980s from an odd
little shop in Kings Cross in Sydney. I think the shopkeeper had
to dust the deck off before he handed it to me. Since then I've
added hundreds of tarot decks to my library, along with many
astrology books — that is my other passion.

After studying with well-known contemporary astrologers,
and studying the founding astrologers, and particularly what is
known as "evolutionary astrology," I began to interpret world
events and themes through the placement of planets in the
zodiac. Often on my channel, an astrology session was followed
by a card reading and the synergy between these two modalities
was uncanny.

I began to see charts as huge jigsaw puzzles, each piece
perfectly fitting the world events humanity was experiencing.
I also began to take my clairvoyance further into mediumship.
I began to reach out to those in the afterlife who may have had
messages for this time. I would catch brief glimpses of their faces

before a reading. I would spend days, even weeks, absorbing and tuning into their vibration before each channeling. Afterwards, it gave me great pleasure to get the validation mediums crave to establish authenticity. Events, and history I would not have known were later revealed after an unscripted and on the spot mediumship session. Like the fact that the late Hollywood star James Dean had a loft cabin which I described in detail, where he often retreated, or that there was an angel-like white entity that crossed some sort of bridge or vortex to talk to Edgar Cayce. That angel-like being was the source of much of the information he brought forward during his channels. Or that Nostradamus scried with colored inks, seeing actual events coming to life in his bowl of water. I was given these pictures through my third eye during the channeling sessions. Similarly, I didn't know that Robin Williams was called to dinner by an elderly lady ringing a bell on what seemed to be the porch of a farmhouse. He would run fast to answer that bell; running fast, like talking fast, thrilled him. I later found out he ran track in high school, including a 1:58.8 in 800 meters in 1969. This same clairvoyance, the pictures I received when I read on world events, was also validated after my readings. It was this accuracy that led to viewers visiting my platforms, subscribing, and returning to them — and something more.

After cancer I was drawn to healing. I had been very focused on healing myself and I somehow knew that my spiritual platforms could become healing places for anyone who was in pain, or fearful, or lonely, or wanting to believe in something more — those searching for answers beyond the mundane or trying to make sense out of chaotic times — just as I had and do now. I began to channel healing messages and, when reading on political and world events, allow the voice of spirit to come through. With trust in the information I was being given, my conscious mind "got out of the way" so that words matched thoughts. I found that many of my viewers were settled after these channelings, and I began to see the purpose of my spiritual odyssey. I had completed a social welfare degree during cancer treatment and graduated in 2017. This degree added to a degree in communications and postgraduate studies in education and community service. It seemed that with my esoteric studies, I became "qualified" to support a mass audience. The long years of orthodox and unorthodox study had a purpose.

Along with astrology, I studied mediumship with two of the more well-known contemporary mediums and undertook an intensive mentorship with an Australian medium. Shaman studies followed and it felt as though I was truly seeing the world around me — not for the first time — but remembering how I interconnected with it during my childhood. I began to understand why I had been so frightened as a child. I had extremely vivid dreams — they were like being lost in a labyrinth. I simply couldn't understand what all the imagery and themes meant. It was like watching a film but being too young to interpret what was in front of me. Some of these dreams involved landscapes that were unfamiliar: women in billowing dresses and bonnets, men in suits and top hats, dusty wagon trails and blazing sun deserts. They weren't modern environments and looking back, it seemed I was stepping through the portals of past lives. I was particularly drawn to America, which later became significant in my work. I have a loyal following in the US and I'm grateful for that support.

Along with the unfathomable and, thus, scary dreams were the energy currents that I would see in front of me, and still do to this day. Imagine seeing an outline in the shape of a person, sensing and feeling someone else in the room, and not knowing what was happening. I ended up hiding under the covers and shutting it out as best I could. However, I could not shut out the knowing and the feeling when I was around other people. It was a keenness of perception and, oftentimes, knowing what they were thinking and feeling. The worst of it was that they often knew that I knew. I'm not good at hiding what I am feeling, and people don't like being so exposed, as I found out repeatedly growing up and into adulthood. I often became an unwitting target for unprovoked attacks, and at the psychic level. Later, I learned ways an empath can protect and defend themselves, in my various voyages into the spirit world and connecting with other empaths, I learned that simple techniques can prevent a world of pain. I never quite got used to that seemingly unprovoked shade from other people who either barely knew me or didn't know me at all. I often wondered: what did I do to them, and to deserve that treatment? It took me many years to work out that I wasn't responsible in any way, including for others' actions. That is entirely their journey to own.

Equally, I found many beautiful connections with people, in fact, more of these magical and synchronistic relationships than not. Whether it was connecting in a very real way with someone "different" from the mainstream, or stumbling upon a kindly person who went out of their way to be nice for an unknown reason, I often felt blessed with my empathy, clairvoyance, and communication. This helped me to remain optimistic about people, society and what could be destined.

I'm not sure why I remain hopeful to this day. It seems to me that there is no other real way to be. The alternative is hopelessness and that is a well of despair. We are always given choices in this earthly life, and they are ours and ours alone to make. When the darkness of despair comes, in the end the choice for me has always been "to look up." I like to think that view is where we see the light, the light of hope.

Chapter 23

Talking with Animals ... and Humans

Animals are a window to your soul and a doorway
to your spiritual destiny. If you let them into your
life and allow them to teach you, you will be better
for it.

Kim Shotola, *The Soul Watchers:*
Animals' Quest to Awaken Humanity

I don't remember a time when I wasn't intuitively connected with
animals. Growing up on a farm, I was riding horses from an early
age, raising poddy lambs, and caring for the many sheepdogs
we had to work our stock. I absolutely loved each one of my pets
and these memories are still bright in my mind's eye while other
childhood memories have dimmed. I guess that's because they
involved the heart. When I moved to be with my husband on his
two-acre property, and began having children, we always had a
dog, cashmere goats and, later, a pony. Birdlife on the property
has always been prolific. I remember the crows cawing as a child
but generally didn't connect with them mentally as I [mistakenly]
associated them with death. It was only later in adulthood that
I began to see them as messengers from the afterlife. This was
further validated when they showed up just before my cancer
diagnosis, following me everywhere and incessantly cawing. It
got so bad, I even asked my meditation group for answers as to
why they followed me everywhere, cawing all the time with what
seemed to be urgency. Had I been more present back then, more in
tune and attuned with my spiritual gifts, I would have understood
they were carrying a warning.

The proliferation of crows everywhere I went was also
accompanied by an increase in clairaudience. I would wake in

the middle of the night to my father's voice shouting my name. This type of clairaudience is not "hearing words or phrases in my mind"; it is like hearing the voice in the physical realm. Again, I was blunt to the implications of these signs. Now, I listen.

It's no accident that animals are highly sensitive and in tune with their environment, they are creatures of survival, just as we can be when we are pushed into extreme threats, such as a cancer diagnosis. I believe we are as connected with animals as we are with humans if we allow ourselves to be. It's a matter of allowing our hearts to take the lead and trusting our intuitive thought processes. While some are more clairvoyant than others, we are all capable of connecting at a deeper level and that is the level that gives us spiritual connection. We all see, hear, think, and feel more than we acknowledge, and more than we allow.

Animals are natural sensitives, as they are closer to the need for survival. I know that dogs, through surviving in a human world, are particularly attuned to our thoughts, and we to them. It's why so many of us are devoted to our dogs because they understand us. A true empath can provide others with that same level of trust. Very good clairvoyants and mediums are sought out for this ability.

Trust. It's a huge word. Within its parameters are loyalty, responsibility, courage, respect, and longevity. Without trust, there is very little left. Our pets place all their trust in us and reward us with their loyalty. They never let us down. Later, when Russia invaded Ukraine in February 2022, my heart broke to see Ukrainian soldiers at the frontlines rescuing the many stray animals displaced by war. These animals often became mascots and one, Patron, a little Jack Russell Terrier attached to the bomb squad, became the mascot of the Ukrainian military. As I watched the tenderness towards these animals, against the backdrop of the brutal march of Vladimir Putin's army, and the epic courage of the Ukrainians, I knew that if God picked a side, it would be with the Ukrainians.

***

When I began my YouTube channel in 2018, the most dangerous politician in the western world in my opinion, Donald Trump, had just been elected. I had watched with dismay as the unthinkable occurred: the Americans were about to elect a man accused of sexual assault (and who had admitted lewd acts on a hot mic on prime-time television), an alleged philanderer and tax dodger, and staunch ally of the Russian war criminal Vladimir Putin, and someone so caught out for lying, few were bothering to keep a tally of his lies — they were so prolific.

The outrage, the world-wide women's marches, the spread of the Trump brand of toxic politics and conspiracy theories to Australia, and a feeling that I had to play a part in some way, do my bit, was the reason I picked up my tarot cards once again and began doing what is known as "political tarot" on my YouTube channel, *Revealing Light: Tarot, Astrology & Spirituality*. These readings allowed me to combine my clairvoyant, psychic and mediumship skills with my journalism and research experience that seemed to guide me to where awareness was needed. It all fitted like a glove. I had always used my "gut instincts" as an investigative journalist and editor — that was what earned me multiple journalism awards — and, indeed, throughout my career to initiate new and successful projects. I had used my hunches and a type of "far-sight" and was rewarded with complex roles on complex projects. Although I didn't know it at the time, that first tarot card spread would lead to a full and satisfying role as a spiritual content creator across multiple social media platforms and one that would help so many of my viewers survive the Trump years in the US.

The channel went from strength to strength, and I began to broaden my readings to include channelings, astrology, and travel and "ghost hunting" vlogging. I kept studying under gifted teachers, mediums, clairvoyants, and astrologers, and like the true Sagittarian (the eternal student) I am, still learning from, and studying with, those I admire.

Over the years I have built a loyal following. My viewers trust the accuracy of my readings. In 2020 I read on Putin and the future of Russia. Some 18 months later in 2022, Putin invaded Ukraine, and the 2020 reading became chillingly accurate. I've lost count of the predictions I've got correct: US, Australian and UK election outcomes, and, most notably, the storming of the US Congress on January 6. Weeks before, I saw a mob at the capital and the image of a diamond drill shattering glass windows. Later, on television coverage, I saw the poles and blunt fashioned weapons breaking the glass of the US Congress windows and the mob breaking through the barriers. It was chilling and unthinkable, yet the reality of the culmination of the Trump years where gaslighting and lies were the norm.

I have a good track record for getting things right in advance, largely due to clairvoyance (the pictures in my head) and intuition. I always think of renowned psychiatrist, the late Dr Carl Jung when explaining how I do what I do: intuition is a combination of gut knowing and analysis and being able to project this around a corner and get it right. In a way, this is only half the answer. Sometimes my predictions just come in a split second. I have no idea how they arrive in my consciousness, just that I have a certainty and confidence they are correct. As Jung says: "In intuition a content presents itself whole and complete, without our being able to explain or discover how this content came into existence."

The clairvoyance is harder to explain. How and why I can see these pictures, I don't really know other than to say it's a God given ability that I don't underestimate because I am always careful not to bring my ego into it. Remaining humble has been a way to keep this gift pure. I know that intuitively.

Another reason my viewers kept returning to my channel was for the paranormal phenomena. From the start, orbs of light would appear on screen, moving visibly through the air while I was reading. One particularly memorable orb in a video which a viewer slowed down, screenshot, and sent me, resembled a small winged and faery-like being. Occasionally, an EPV (Electronic Voice Phenomenon) can be heard during recordings. I remember one while I was telling my viewers about my close friend who took his own life, the friend I talk about in the first part of this book. "I never got to say goodbye," I said. It was at this time when viewers said they heard a male voice say "goodbye." Other EPVs have used the name my parents and sisters and brothers use for me, "Mary." Of course, I know who these voices are; they are my parents and sister who are now in spirit, reaching out through my recording devices to let me know they are still around me.

Healing has been a huge theme of my YouTube channel and the social media platforms that support it. I channel deep psychological, spiritual and well-being messages, and I bring insight during turbulence that provides a holistic lens through which my viewers can make sense of a chaotic world. I have no doubt we are here on this earth, and in this lifetime, to learn and evolve. Evolution is always in motion, and it may not be linear, yet the destination is always, always to learn the lesson. Once learnt, the need for the lesson falls away and resolution occurs. New pathways and "timelines" also tend to follow the resolution of old karma.

I am very grateful to be able to provoke insight and reflection in my viewers. I believe that this ability is linked to my desire to help those who come my way with gratitude and kindness in their hearts, and to my own battle against cancer when I had to learn to heal myself. Cancer survivors who get that second chance at life will tell you that you must dig deep within your soul to heal from cancer and, as the possibility of recurrence is always there, the lessons must be fully experienced and understood.

Cancer also places a boundary against repeating old lessons, habits, and karmic cycles. It's a life-changing lesson as many have experienced.

Cancer survivors are healing experts. Individuals within the collective are compelled towards those who have something of value to offer them during their time of learning. One of our biggest life challenges is illness and dying. We all experience both, one way or another, in the end. Telling my cancer story was not only liberating for me, but it also attracted those human beings that had either been through a similar experience or had deep compassion and understanding for someone who had. Now there is a community of like-minded individuals who make up the Revealing Light channel. I believe that what I offer is a channel, or frequency that became more tuned-in as a result of my cancer and facing my mortality. That experience broke through my lack of awareness; the veil that I had put up between worlds out of fear and misunderstanding. Once that was broken, access to the higher realms revealed a dazzling and life-changing light.

Chapter 24

The Blueprint in Astrology

A physician without a knowledge of Astrology has
no right to call himself a physician.

Hippocrates

As well as clairvoyance, mediumship and tarot, astrology has
been a mainstay of my esoteric practices. I had always been
interested in the zodiac and my rudimentary understanding
and knowledge had allowed for a good understanding of the
personality traits of all signs, however, I didn't begin to study
astrology in earnest until one of my YouTube viewers took me
under her wing. She was a gifted astrologist and saw something
in me that gave her confidence that I would make an able
student. She sent me her astrology books, collected over the
decades, and began to teach me the foundations of astrology:
signs, houses of the zodiac, planets, and aspects. I began to
see — and feel — universal pictures emerge within charts, along
with strong evolutionary themes. Natal charts appeared in my
mind's eye as giant jigsaw puzzles that spanned lifetimes. This
could not be accidental, I thought, these themes so obvious in
our earthly existence with threads to the heavens, and to what I
refer to as spirituality.

It led me to research and study Evolutionary Astrology
(EA) through courses that had been based on the work of
the late Jeffrey Wolf Green, widely attributed as the founder
of EA. At the same time, I began to read the astrology books
that all students consume: contemporary astrologers whose
work informs modern-day astrology practice, and fine tuning
with further studies to strengthen foundational knowledge. I
believe I will always be learning astrology and to a Sagittarian

who loves to learn, who has accumulated double degrees and postgraduate diplomas from top universities in Australia, the study of astrology is just as rewarding and sustaining.

One of the first things astrologers learn is how to read a natal chart. Importantly, the nodes of the moon are a focus, as is the position and sign of Pluto (to EA astrologers, Pluto and the nodes of the moon are paramount as they indicate the "evolution" of the soul in past and present lifetimes).

As I learned to think like an astrologer, my own natal chart revealed many stories. Themes, lessons, strengths, vulnerabilities, and patterns began to emerge. I looked at the charts of my family and saw that patterns and stories were interwoven with mine. How could this be? As I learned with other esoteric sciences there are deep reservoirs of truth in our existence on this earth, in our humanity and in our connection to the divine. Astrology illuminates all of this in a map that our earthly eyes, mind, and intuition can interpret. Astrology is not merely academic; it is also about where we focus and how we interpret charts. While foundational knowledge is similar amongst astrologers, interpretation and emphasis is not. I find I often read a chart intuitively, allowing my perception to expand beyond foundations and across time. A past, present, and future theme will often be revealed and explain why there is conflict between planets and signs in a natal chart. These conflicts, or "squares" as they are known also reveal the potential for our greatest achievements, or lost opportunities, in this lifetime. I often say that if I had been an astrologer 40 years ago, I would have sidestepped much of the drama and disappointment of this lifetime. However, I have also learned there is divine timing in everything. Who am I to rewrite history? I will get that opportunity, perhaps, in my next lifetime.

My own astrological blueprint in this lifetime reveals major issues with my health and when I examine my chart and the transits of 2015 — the year I was diagnosed with cancer — I see and hear a whirring red siren that screamed health crisis. My blueprint and purpose, along with my 360 turnarounds, from orthodox career to spiritual counselor is also there. Let's take a look.

Health in the Natal Chart

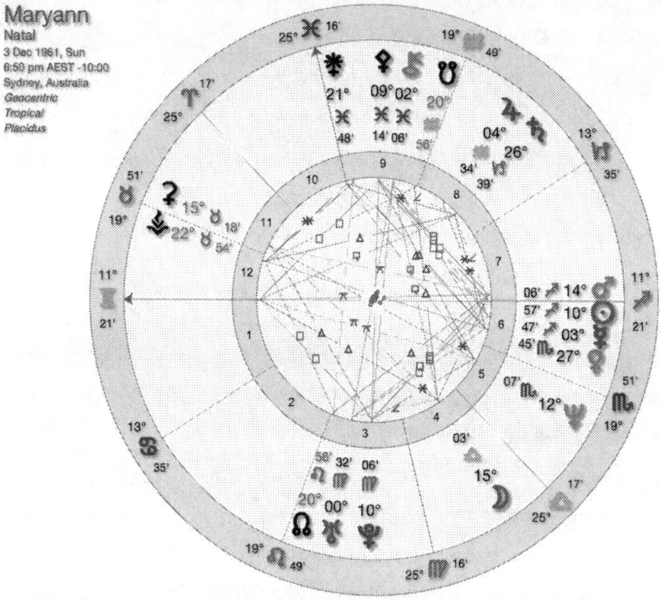

Image 1: Natal astrology chart.

*My natal chart — note the activity in the Sixth House (health) and Third House (communication) and Chiron (wounded healer) in Pisces (intuition) the Ninth House (learning).

As I was later to find out in life and post-cancer, astrology can help provide indications of the major themes that you will face in your lifetime. In my own chart, I have multiple planets in Sagittarius in the Sixth House. For those who do not know, the Sixth House is the House that rules, among other things, health. It also incorporates service to others, daily routines, and work.

These areas also provide me with some insight into the past. I won't say they led to my cancer, but they may have predisposed me to cancer. It's not some magical answer. However, the truth is I am, and have always been, a workaholic. Work is integral to who I am. It helps define me. I am a creator, always on a quest for self-knowledge and experience. I have used work over the years to quench my thirst for new horizons, learnings, relationship development and, unfortunately, to prove my worth. Conjunct, my sun in Sagittarius in the Sixth House, is Mercury. Mercury is the planet of inner and outer communication. Sagittarius is the sign that rules the Ninth House in the zodiac. Sagittarius is associated with higher knowledge, learning, travel, wanderlust, logic, and spirituality. It's also the sign associated with law and religion. In the Sixth House, my Sagittarius sun is conjunct my Mercury, and conjunct, my Mars (action, drive), which strays just over into the Seventh House (relationships and partnerships). My Sagittarius sun meant that, in a way, I knew no boundaries when it came to my work and my career. Work and service to others are what defined me.

The learning for me was looking at the aspects in my chart. Curiously, those planets, squared Uranus and Pluto in the Third House (communications). My Third House straddles both in Leo and in Virgo. Uranus and Pluto are conjunct within 10 degrees of each other in Virgo. My North node in the Third House is in Leo. The Third House is primarily associated with communication. It was no accident that I came into this lifetime, a writer, a communicator and a podcast and video content maker. All these activities have felt right. They are the foundation of my creativity. Over the years I have written for newspapers, both state and regional. I have led national communication campaigns for government and the private sector. I have written ministerial speeches and contributed to Prime Ministers' speeches. I have developed many, many communication strategies for national organizations, government, and overseas not-for-profit organizations. My lifetime career in communications has been extremely rewarding. I have also self-published books and have had my work picked up by publishing companies prior to cancer. After cancer, as many of you know through reading this book, my communication mode changed. I went from written communications in the main, to producing video and audio spiritual content. When I look at my natal chart, this was always going to be one of my timelines. My Pluto in Virgo sextiles (harmonious flow), my Neptune in Scorpio. This gives me a depth of self-expression and, given the choice, spirituality. Pluto is the planet of deep, deep dives toward the hidden truth. Neptune in Scorpio in my Fifth House (expression and creativity) indicates that I will be exploring the nebulous realms of what is coming into form and what is passing away. Everyone born between the 1940s–2030s has this sextile in their natal chart. It is an evolutionary aspect which gives us all the opportunity to forge a spiritual connection and create the vision of what we will experience in life, though not all choose to use it.

My Uranus, the planet of rebellion, and often lightning-quick change, squares my Mercury in Sagittarius, in my Sixth House. I am rarely predictable, even to those closest to me.

Back to the health aspect of my natal chart and how this may have indicated an issue with my health. The planets in my Third House in Virgo indicate that I will always strive to prove myself. Virgo is all about the detail; it's all about the work, and it can also be about needing to prove yourself. Virgo is always about becoming more than what you think you are. The communication has always been constant in my lifetime, indicating that one of the ways I define my self-worth is through communicating, and learning to encompass the detail. In my case, this detail extends to universal truth and the higher realms and how they interact, influence and impact on our earthly existence. Did I mention my husband and my eldest son are Virgos? Nothing is by chance. I learn from them, and they learn from me.

I want to talk also about Venus in Scorpio in the Sixth House right alongside my sun and Mercury in Sagittarius. Venus represents love. It can also represent inner and outer values, and some even associate it with destiny. Venus in Scorpio is not necessarily a beneficial placement. Venus is the planet of love, and it is in its detriment in intense and complex Scorpio. That is not always a bad thing because it means that I develop very deep and meaningful relationships during my lifetime. When you add Mars in Sagittarius in the Seventh House of relationships, I have been both blessed and wounded in relationships. Those intense, passionate, and committed relationships have exposed the wound patterns that I brought into this lifetime. They have led me to isolate myself, and take those deep, introspective dives to figure things out. To examine the lessons, and to learn. Incidentally, this is where the asteroid Hygeia is placed. Hygeia is associated with health.

We all have complexities in our natal charts. Venus in Scorpio in my Sixth House meant that not only did I give my all to my creative work, I also gave my all to my relationships. Often, this was to the detriment of my own health and well-being. When you add in my moon in Libra (balance and justice) in the Fourth House of home and security, I was sometimes the proverbial Don Quixote, tilting at windmills, fighting battles that most people might ignore and those that couldn't be won without great cost to myself. Like everyone else, I've spent a lifetime learning the lessons. That is how we evolve.

I also want to mention my Saturn in Capricorn in the Eighth House that is a particularly difficult placement for me, because it meant that I was often working for others. It sits alongside my Jupiter in Aquarius in the Eighth House. The Eighth House is ruled by Pluto (death and rebirth) and is associated with the sign of Scorpio. It embodies strong themes of transformation. Add that to Chiron in Pisces in my Ninth House, the Ninth House being higher knowledge, and Pisces, being one of the most psychic signs in the zodiac, and I start to see some purpose behind my health crisis in this lifetime, and what would emerge from it.

The Day of my major surgery

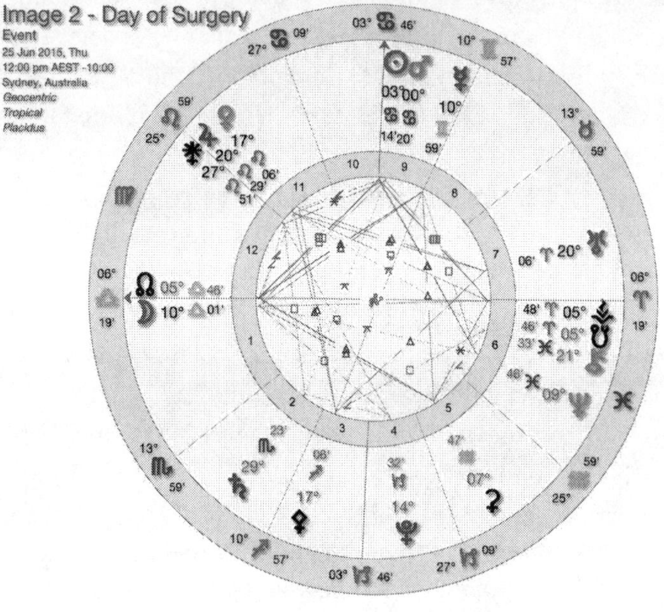

Image 2: Day of Surgery

*Note the Trines and Sextiles (harmonious flows and beneficial aspects), the Grand Trines (potential for accomplishment, talent, and ability) in my surgery chart, along with the T-Squares (tension leads to new approaches). It was never going to be easy but, perhaps, luck was on my side.

I want to talk a little bit about the astrology of the day of my surgery. It was scheduled for June 25, 2015. I had just finished almost seven weeks of radiation and chemotherapy before my surgery, and I was apprehensive to say the least, about what was in front of me. I was to face a six and a half-hour surgery, complicated by the position of my tumor in my pelvis. Even drawing up the chart of the day was difficult for me. It is very telling and there are some very powerful astrological aspects.

Looking back at that perilous time, those aspects are, almost, miraculous. The first thing I see are the trines. These are beneficial aspects in the astrological chart. The harmonious flows, or help from the heavens, doesn't stop there. I have a trine from the moon (the soul, feelings) just inside the First House in Libra (justice, balance) to Mercury in Gemini (communication) in the Ninth House of learning, education, and higher thinking. There is also a trine from the North Node (purpose) in the Twelfth House to Mercury. Something is ending and something is beginning on this day. Perhaps my soul is reborn on this day, certainly altered and there was no doubt that the removal of the cancer during this operation gave me a second chance in life.

There is another trine from Uranus (the unexpected, lightening change) in Aries in the Seventh House of partnerships to Venus (what we value, love) and lucky Jupiter in the Eleventh House of networks and groups. This tells me that my surgical team were able to competently handle any unexpected obstacles that arose in the surgery. There is yet another trine from Neptune (something coming into form) in Pisces (intuition) in the Sixth House of health, public service, and work to the sun (I am) and Mars (action and drive) in the Ninth House of logic, education, knowledge. Again, my surgeon and his team were exceptional, and I was lucky to be in such gifted hands.

These favorable astrological aspects on the day of my surgery tell me that this was an event on a certain date in time, and at a certain place, that was destined to alter my life with the North Node in the Twelfth House of endings and my moon in the First House of beginnings. I would even go as far as saying that the outcome of the operation, though complex and difficult, had every chance of being favorable.

Chiron, the wounded healer, was also in Pisces (intuition, spirituality) in the Sixth House (health). Chiron was sitting alongside Neptune (spirituality) in that Sixth House. Something was emerging and coming into form, and I believe that was a new chance for health and healing, and the spiritual work I would do in the future.

However, this surgery was also extremely difficult as indicated by the T-square and the squares from the moon and North Node to the conjunct sun with Mars (action, drive) in Cancer (feelings) in the Ninth House. The surgeon was forced to draw on his knowledge and skill, but also on his gut feelings when confronted with the unexpected.

My surgeon, very well known in his field for his expertise in my type and placement of cancer, told me early in my treatment that with surgery "we are going for cure." When he checked in on me post-operatively, he said that it was a very difficult surgery, and one that required tremendous skill, and something else: he said that at one point he didn't know whether he could proceed with his plan for my surgery, and whether he had to divert in another direction, however, he called it luck beyond his skill. "It was like the stars were aligned for you."

Other aspects in this chart further indicate the difficulty of the surgery. Saturn in Scorpio (endings and beginnings) is the hard task master and this giant planet which demands the hard yards for success, was forming a quincunx (incompatibility) to the sun/Mars conjunction. My operation would not have been possible without modern surgical techniques. I would have a long road of recovery, and I did. It was perhaps also hinting that this surgery would alter my body, and my life, considerably.

I had spent many years studying and learning to establish and progress my career. At the time of the surgery I believed, mistakenly, I could simply resume my old life. The chart and the aspects demonstrate that what they did in that surgery would have consequences for my physical body going forward. This type of surgery had an impact on my physical body. There is what is known as an inconjunct between Neptune in Pisces in the Sixth House — remembering the Sixth House rules health, and it can be where illness shows up, and the moon in the First House of beginnings. There was the end of a cycle in the North Node in the Twelfth House and a new way of living indicated in this chart. It took me a long, long time to re-emerge into society post-cancer surgery. Yes, between radiation chemotherapy and surgery, my physical strength was very much diminished, and it was impossible to go back to my old life. Having said that, what awaited was a beginning.

I want to go back to the trine between Neptune (spirituality) in the Sixth House of health and work, and the sun and Mars in the Ninth House of education, logic, higher thinking, and publishing. With Mercury also in this Ninth House, I would later write about my cancer battle. The surgery provided me with a lifetime of experience and allowed me to begin to be of service to others in a way that would bring all that I had learned through cancer and loss to others and to forge new partnerships and relationships. The second trine involves Uranus in the Seventh House to Jupiter and Venus in the Eleventh House of networks, groups, and community. This operation radically changed my life and my relationships and gave me experiences to bring to my networks and social media communities in the future.

The trine from the moon (the soul, the mother, feelings) in Libra in the First House to Mercury in Gemini in the Ninth House (learning, publishing) was an indication of where my soul's journey was taking me. I would communicate with a depth of understanding of death and rebirth that I didn't have before my illness.

I believe the surgery also challenged me to let go of my old life and embrace a new spiritual one. In recognizing, accepting, and strengthening my psychic and clairvoyant abilities, and speaking out about them and through them, I was doing what I came here to do. Such is the power of these major events and, in astrology, the transits of the planets through the zodiac, to change the course of our lives. We should not step back from these life-changing events however difficult. The learning which brings understanding and awareness, will carry us forward to new destinations and horizons we could not have imagined before.

There is one final intuition on this chart and it concerns my mother who passed away in 2010. My mother was the quintessential Capricorn, hardworking, a problem solver and leader. She was a registered nurse known for her expertise, particularly in a time of crisis. In this chart, Pluto (power, the underworld, hidden depths) in the Fourth House (home, family, and the mother) squares the Libran moon in the First House. Was my mother helping me from the afterlife in that six and a half-hour operation to achieve the justice of a second chance and a new beginning in life? I like to think so.

I want to talk briefly about my Solar Return chart for 2014–2015. I was diagnosed in January 2015, so this is a chart worth analysing. 2014 was a tumultuous year for me, with my boss, colleague, mentor, and good friend taking his own life. I talk about this in the first section of this book. When I look at this Solar Return chart, I am immediately drawn to the Eighth House with its conglomeration of planets. The Eighth House, as you may now know, is the House of endings, transformation, and new beginnings. It is also the House most associated with loss, grief, death and dying. My sun and Mercury are conjunct in Sagittarius, with a focus on communication (Mercury) and learning (Sagittarius) about loss and letting go. Venus (love, and what we value) is also in this House, along with Saturn in Scorpio. This is a story of great change, endings and new beginnings. With Saturn (task master) in Scorpio (the traditional ruler of the Eighth House), it is clear I will need to work hard to let go of an old cycle. With my moon (feelings, the soul) on the ascendant in Taurus (determination), I would be in this battle to end one way of living and find a new, more stable, way forward, and for the long haul.

Solar return 2014/2015

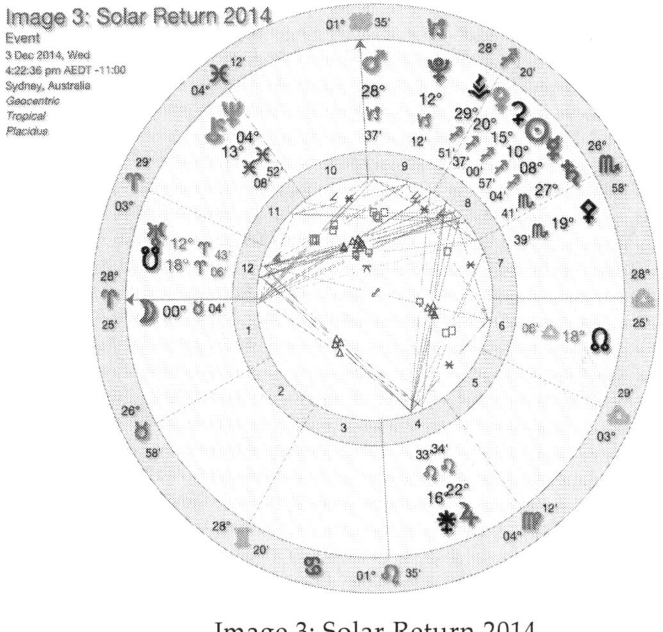

Image 3: Solar Return 2014

*Solar Return (important influences & themes) for the year of diagnosis, surgery, and treatment in 2014–2015. So much change, including lightning endings and changes in my work, relationships, and partnerships.

These planets, Saturn, Mercury and the sun, in this Eighth House were squaring my Chiron (the Wounded Healer) in Pisces in the Eleventh House, and Neptune (something coming into form) in Pisces, also in the Eleventh House. The Eleventh House represents networks, groups and communities, indicating my relationships and networks were all undergoing tremendous conflict and change. The fact that these squares were to a Chiron and Neptune conjunction in Pisces, the most intuitive, psychic, and spiritual sign in the zodiac, perhaps portended the possibility of not only joining but creating new spiritual communities. I was confused at the time about what and why I had been diagnosed with cancer. I had shut down my intuition and clairvoyance over the years, and I was ignoring all the signs from the universe that something was very wrong, and that disaster loomed. Yet it was precisely the transformation needed to put me on a new and spiritual path.

It's relevant to look at where Pluto was in this Solar Return. Radical and transforming Pluto along with Mars (action, drive), were in my Ninth House (learning) in Capricorn (leadership, resilience and hard work). Pluto was squaring Uranus (change) in Aries (new beginnings and identity) in the Twelfth House of endings, along with the South Node (what we need to let go of), perhaps indicating that the loss of the life I knew would bring forward a new way of living. This is further demonstrated with action-oriented Mars squaring my moon in Taurus. This radical change was soul driven.

In summary, my old life and career were ending, and something new was forming, driven largely by that Neptune and Chiron in Pisces in the Eleventh House and powerful and evolutionary Pluto squaring Uranus and the South Node in the Twelfth House of endings.

However, just as my old life was falling away, I also had a trine between Ceres (new growth) and Uranus (change), and lucky and expansive Jupiter in Leo (creativity, self-expression) in the Fourth House (home and family). Communication oriented Mercury and my Sun are also trining Uranus and the South Node in that Twelfth House. Nowadays, my work is home based, unlike my previous career which took me to destinations and communities across Australia. Somehow, what was to come would bring new relationships and partnerships into my life, focused on the spiritual and involving virtual communities located across the world.

I didn't know it then, but years later I have a thriving spiritual audience that arose from the evolution I experienced because of my illness.

Solar return 2015/2016

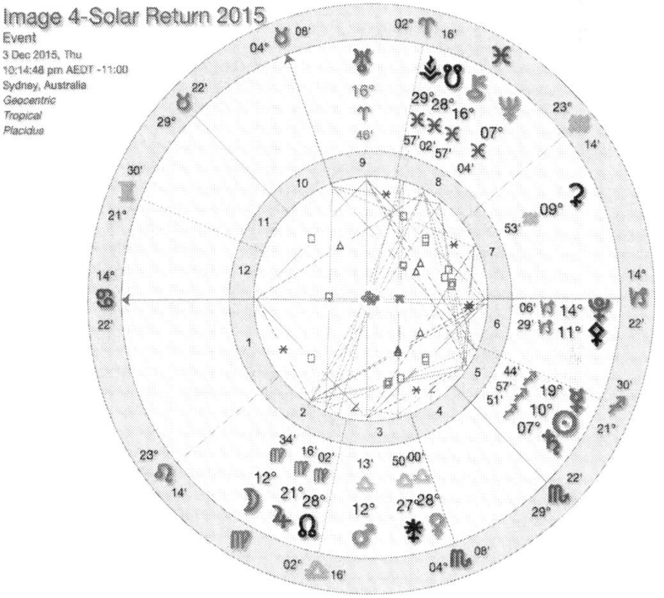

Image 4: Solar Return 2015

*Treatment and recovery. Neptune, Chiron and the South Node all in Pisces have moved into the Eighth House of endings and beginnings, and transformation. My Sagittarius sun is in the Fifth House of creativity and self-expression. Even during this Solar Return, and active treatment and recovery, I was readying for a complete 360 change of direction.

I also want to look at my Solar Return for the 2015–16 year because I was undertaking mop-up chemotherapy and healing from major and life altering surgery. Would you be surprised to hear that there are T-Squares dominating this chart? There are oppositions between the moon (feelings, the soul) in Virgo in the Second House of finances to Chiron and Neptune in Pisces in the Eighth House. There are also oppositions between Jupiter (luck and expansion) in hardworking and detail-oriented Virgo in that Second House to Chiron in Pisces in the Eighth House. This indicates the challenges of this time with changes in finances and career but also that these changes were part of my Soul's journey. Chiron in psychic Pisces in my natal chart and in my Solar Return charts will always indicate where the energy of healing is needed. In this chart it was in letting go of my old career and the identity that was created through that, to begin new work which involved using my clairvoyant and psychic abilities, and in the service to others.

The challenge was to bring something new forward, drawing on my dormant spiritual abilities. The Square from Jupiter to the planet of communication, Mercury in Sagittarius, in the Fifth House of creativity and self-expression meant I was challenged to learn about my treatment to recover, and to eventually share these learnings with others.

There is also another hard aspect: an Opposition between transformational Pluto and the ascendant Cancer (emotions and feelings). As any cancer survivor will tell you, treatment is a roller coaster ride. There were times of great depression yet also triumph, and achievement. These powerful experiences were psychologically and spiritually transformational.

Hard won achievement can come from great conflict and this is shown in the proliferation of planets squaring each other in this chart. The moon squaring Saturn (hard work) in the Fifth house in Sagittarius, as well as my sun (essence of who we are) in Sagittarius indicates this was a period of incredible learning about my soul's purpose and how to express this through my career and public image. At the time I was writing the first part of this book — confirmation that sharing and communicating my experiences could one day help others. The sun and Saturn are conjunct, while Mercury (communication) in Sagittarius in the Fifth House is conjunct my sun. There is a blending of energies and impacts in all conjunctions. A new and more fulfilling career was coming into form as I used my experiences and my recovery to write this book and develop a new way of working which incorporated all my experiences and focused on spiritual connection and the soul's journey. I wrote the first part of this book in real time as I healed from what was a cornerstone physical, psychological and, importantly, spiritual event in my life — one that changed my life forever.

Writing the book challenged me to share my story when I was at my most vulnerable. That took a level of courage.

All cancer warriors and survivors undergo tremendous change in career and finances. This is shown in this chart as I adapted what was a mainstream and managerial career into one that was largely spiritual, and in the service of others. This Solar Return is a chart of metamorphosis driven by profound change, challenges, and obstacles in healing and in continuing to work, albeit in a reduced capacity.

In 2015 I worked as a consultant from home, part-time, as I healed from surgery and continued mop-up chemotherapy. However, what was coming into form with Neptune and Chiron in Pisces in the Eighth House, was a new way of working, which drew on my dormant clairvoyant and psychic abilities. Uranus in Aries in the Ninth House of learning, logic and the higher mind, indicates the learning I was undergoing as a result of radical change in my life.

The challenge for any of us experiencing major life change is to learn and evolve, and to journey inward to find that creative center which allows self-expression and connection with others.

This can be a life altering journey which can manifest deep spirituality and usher in new meaning and purpose.

***

It's almost sunset when I write this today, in 2023. So much was in the astrology when I look back at the years covering diagnosis, surgery, treatment, and recovery, including in the Sixth House (health), the Ninth House which includes publishing and in the Twelfth House of endings and First House of new cycles. The workings of my natal Neptune in Scorpio and the influences of transiting Neptune in Pisces and natal and transiting Chiron in Pisces, were the signatures of my metamorphosis into the nebulous realms of something being healed (Chiron, wounded healer), the realization of my blueprint as a healer, and the way my clairvoyant and psychic abilities "switched on" to take me on a new road, one that I could never have imagined I would travel all those years ago during my orthodox career in journalism, government and as a senior consultant. Yes, my relationships did change. Many colleagues and friends fell away, either because of my isolation and illness, or because people wondered what I was doing as a clairvoyant and astrologer on YouTube.

There were many friendships that stood the test of time. Those friends and family who were not surprised by the fork in the road and new destination. People you are close to generally know, and believe in, the "real you."

I believe that astrology and all the divination tools, including the imagery and archetypes of the tarot, can help enlighten, and connect, people to the sacred knowledge within. They can be the keys that unlock the vault of learning, and they can give much needed perspective to the "why" in our lives.

Bad things do happen to people; they happened to me but seen in the context of this lifetime, they have taught me integral spiritual and karmic truths. I have become self-aware in a way that takes me above this earthly life and into the realms of understanding and acceptance, and connection to the Divine, the Creator of all things.

Chapter 25

Chiron the Wounded Healer

The wound is where the light enters you.

Rumi

On January 4, 2023, the moon was sextile (harmony and flow) Chiron. The sun was also squaring (conflicting) Chiron. Depending on when you're reading this there will be different astrological movements and patterns and aspects, but I want to talk a little bit more about Chiron because I believe the placement of Chiron in our astrology charts tells us about one of the most important aspects of our life's purpose: healing and where and how that thread of healing runs through our lives.

For those who know nothing about astrology, Chiron is the wounded healer. Chiron was named after the centaur in Greek mythology who was a healer and teacher, however, he could not heal himself. We all have Chiron in our charts and wherever this placement is, there you will find an indication of your own greatest healing powers, and the source of your own wound. In my natal chart, Chiron is in Pisces (empathetic, mystical, intuition, psychic senses) in my Ninth House which is the home of Sagittarius (learning, higher knowledge, intellectual and spiritual adventurers) which explains why I ended up using my psychic abilities in a career which metamorphosed post-cancer journey. I encourage you to find a good astrologer and have a look at where your Chiron is placed in your natal chart; what sign and House because it will reveal a lot about the kind of patterns that recur and are present in your lifetime. For me, Chiron in Pisces in my Ninth House tells me that both intuition and analysis will guide me. Equally, I can recall many, many times in my life where I didn't trust my intuition even though it screamed at me for attention. I wasn't confident enough in my own strength back then even though I knew with every fiber of my being that something beyond (or within) myself was pulling me in such a way that I couldn't ignore. I just couldn't necessarily explain that to anyone else in logical ways. As I navigated my way through cancer diagnosis and treatment in 2015, I drew on my intuition and quest for knowledge to devise a map of how I would travel through tough treatment to reach a destination of "cured." Sometimes I used logic, other times intuition. It was a complete inner and outer process to heal and learn. After cancer and confronting my mortality, I learned to trust my intuition.

So here is what I want you to do today: find out where your Chiron is and address the wound because you shouldn't need to go through a lifetime not understanding who you are, what your blueprint is in this lifetime, and how you can find your strength by understanding your weakness, your Achilles heel. Most importantly, understanding and becoming confident in your ability to connect deeply with others through your own experiences with your wound patterns, because Chiron shows us where we have healing powers due to our own deep spiritual wounds.

Sometimes you can best connect with your intuition by asking what is it that I need to know today and by feeling into that intuition and that emotion hunch. That's when you can apply your logic to it. I know the two don't necessarily fit, but if your logical, conscious mind is telling you to do one thing and your intuition is screaming at you to do another, what are you going to do? You are not going to sabotage yourself by ignoring that huge voice in your head, and in your heart, because you fear whatever the warning is your intuition is allowing you to see in that present moment. If you ignore that screaming voice within, you simply sabotage yourself.

We don't need to live constantly and permanently with our wound patterns. Make a choice to take advantage of, and receive, the gift that spirit has given you, the gift of healing. That is your birth right.

Some of our most powerful intuitions will arise with matters of the heart. I believe that intuition, psychic senses, were given to us as a highly evolved navigational tool to move through this lifetime. It is the one thing that can lead to our independence because it is the highly evolved part of us; that spiritual "know how" and connection, that most of us aren't even aware is there.

What do I mean by "living a spiritual life"? Well, this is living life with a reliable, stable, resilient, active, dialogue with the inner self. It is what connects us with spirit, with passed over loved ones, with the upper world, and with realms that we can't see, touch, feel if we are living only a mundane, earthly existence. We weren't meant to be so limited. Instead, we were always destined to learn how to develop our inner and psychic senses.

Our fears stop us from living that divine, spiritual connection. It's a connection that gives us so much more. It allows us to navigate tough times, and to manifest as much abundance as we are capable of in that present moment. It's also our fear of loss of control; loss of that concreteness that is so associated with mundane living, that stops us from fully embracing the spiritual beings that we are and that we are meant to be.

At any given moment, we can embark on a magical journey of living spiritually. We can step forward into that journey without knowing where we are putting our feet, because intuition is our guide. Learning to hone that intuition, to fully utilize that intuition, is what will likely guarantee our steps forward in an unknown territory.

I urge everybody who might be reading this regardless of the time, the place, the year, to take that leap of faith, to see the world through the child's eyes and navigate their way forward into a spiritual life. You will not find instability, rather, stability. Being your own spiritual guide will ensure you have everything you need, including the healing of any ancestral patterns and you will have your opportunity to understand your vulnerabilities, the lessons that you need to learn. This is when you begin to evolve into a spiritual being and one who lives a spiritual life.

Chapter 26

The Art of Divination

The true Tarot is symbolism; it speaks no other language and offers no other signs.

A. E. Waite

As I write this, the sun is conjunct (alongside and a blending of energies) Pluto, and the moon is trining (harmonious flow) Pluto. The sun is the center of our solar system. It is the lifeforce and the essence, and the action that takes us forward. Pluto is power, often what is hidden, often what can be corrupted, and can represent our deepest truths, choices, and values. To me this is a perfect time to explain why I love the tarot. I have been familiar with the tarot since I was a young adult. My first deck was the Aquarian Tarot by [the late] David Palladini. I'm not sure why I was drawn to the tarot. Perhaps it was my clairvoyance, perhaps the artist within, and perhaps the obvious and not so obvious psychology of the tarot. When I receive messages from Spirit, they come in the form of pictures and symbols. This is what is at the heart of the tarot; archetypes that represent our journey in life. As I deal the cards in a reading, they stimulate my clairvoyance, and my clairaudience. There is something else though. It is something that I cannot explain logically. However, if I look for an explanation, which is magical or even describes the Jungian term of synchronicity, I can arrive at a simple truth. This truth is rooted in the same place that my clairvoyance arises. How can a set of cards predict the future? On their own, they can't. In the hands of an intuitive, and better still, a clairvoyant, and a psychic medium, cards can become extremely powerful in divination.

Cards can reveal universal truths. Tarot can mirror life's journey. This journey is not linear, nor is the Major Arcana in the tarot linear, yet progression in the tarot is broken down into major life experiences that drive us forward; that have the potential for evolution of the soul. Tarot cards are far more than just the basic meaning assigned by the most well-known tarot deck in the world, the Rider Waite. Meaning is interpreted by the reader and is based on his/her relationship with the tarot, and the strength of divination abilities. That is why no two tarot readers will get the same result when reading on the same question. The best tarot readers understand the spiritual and universal nature of the tarot. The best tarot readers are accurate and mostly correct in their predictions. That is the yardstick.

For me, reading cards, generates those clairvoyant visions, and expands access, and use of, my subconscious mind. As Jung reminds us, the subconscious mind is a vast reservoir, which can reveal the complexity, yet simplicity, of our spiritual lives. We are far more than what we think.

The imagination for me has always been a tool to access my subconscious but imagination differs from clairvoyance in that clairvoyance is instantaneous, unbidden and involves connection between an earthly and afterlife realities.

In my younger years, I placed the concreteness of the conscious mind over my subconscious mind. The cancer journey, broke through that hardness to allow the flow of that subconscious reservoir into my daily life, and now through my spiritual platforms.

I often look back at my early career, and now know why I was successful in bringing forward the stories, the policies, and the messages that resonated with people. As a young journalist I was often breaking stories before everybody else. I acted on what I thought were my hunches. In hindsight, they were tied to my intuition and clairvoyance.

I want to say something here about communication, about words, and about the way we send and receive communication. What social science fails to illuminate in the communication model is how we listen intuitively, and how we speak from the heart, and from that great reservoir of the subconscious. That is why so many of us identify with the images in the tarot and the Major Arcana.

Let's examine the Major Arcana.

The Major Arcana is the world's most famous tarot deck, the Rider Waite, begins with the Fool embarking on a journey. The Fool (associated with the lightning change that Uranus brings) has only a bare minimum of possessions, a swag, a white rose (which to me represents innocence) and, in some decks, the faithful, loyal dog at his/her heels. The sun is at the Fool's back. As we look closely at the card, the Fool is in danger of a misstep, which would send him/her over a cliff. Yet, the Fool is eager to begin his/her journey. In astrology, the sun is associated with action, and the moon with feeling. Here the sun's presence tells us that it is action that the Fool is most concerned with on the journey.

I can relate this card to how I dealt with cancer. When I was diagnosed, I had no idea, whether I would survive nor know what the surgery and treatment would mean for me. Yet, I was motivated and determined to take those steps into the unknown. I researched everything I could about cancer and its treatment. I familiarized myself with the surgical procedure I would undergo. However, while that knowledge mitigated some of the fear, I had to draw on my spiritual relationship with God to face the trials I would experience. I remember consulting with a well-known Australian psychic before the operation, and these three words that she impressed upon me really took me through that major surgery. She said, "You will be fine." My intuition and my blind faith, like that of the Fool, allowed me to overcome my fear the night before the operation, and throughout the long wait in pre-surgery before the surgeon began the operation.

The next card in the Major Arcana is the Magician, associated with the planet Mercury which rules both Virgo and Gemini. The Magician has every ace up his sleeve. The Magician is grounded; the Magician has the strength of his heart and the power of his feelings, the truth of his sword and the wand of his passion and motivation to manifest new starts. The inherent strengths we all possess come to the fore when we are faced with crisis. I learnt that we have many gifts and abilities at our disposal if we can only believe in them. When we believe in them, we begin to manifest our future.

Alongside the Magician is his counterpart, the High Priestess. In astrology she is associated with the moon and therefore the sign of Cancer, however, she is also linked strongly with all the water signs including psychic Pisces. She holds the book of all spiritual knowledge in some decks, and she is often depicted with the moon at her feet. It is often said that the feelings reside in our subconscious, the Moon in the tarot being associated with our emotions. She is divine intuition. She is the perfect channel between the Divine within, and God/Great Spirit. I drew on both the Magician and the High Priestess archetypes during my cancer experience. The knowledge that I gained from that blueprint event in this lifetime is directly responsible for the work that I do today.

The Empress is the archetype associated with the mother. In astrology she is associated with Venus, the planet of Love and with the sign of Taurus. The Empress is determined. She plants her crops in the knowledge that within a season of time, abundance will be hers. She sits alongside the Emperor which is associated with the astrological sign of Aries. The Emperor is a culmination of all four kings in the tarot. The Emperor is wise and deserves his seat on a throne that represents mastery and control. Random events will always come into our lives. They are the challenges that we were not anticipating. They are the events which call us to question and ask: Why? However, when we get to a level of wisdom, we can restore, or create, order out of chaos.

The next card in the tarot is the Hierophant, and perhaps one of my favorite cards in the deck. The traditional meaning of the Hierophant is the higher order — some see it as representing courts, governments, legal challenges, religion. I see the Hierophant as the direct conduit to Spirit, who has the final say. When those challenging events are spiralling out of control, look to your faith, your belief, and your hope because the Hierophant embodies all of these. And as much as this card represents Spirit, the Hierophant also represents your own divinity. Time and time again, when I was experiencing the challenges of negotiating my cancer journey, I was also experiencing the greatest affirmation of my faith in God. In the tarot, the Hierophant has his hand stretched in a symbol of decree. The Hierophant is also associated in astrology with the sign of Taurus. The Hierophant is determined and will not be put off, and those affected by this decree understand that, in the end, whatever journey you are embarking on, has already been written.

The Lovers card follows the Hierophant and is associated with the astrological sign of Gemini. I am reminded every day, that yes, we can live in solitude, but our lifetimes, and our learnings, are defined by our relationships. Our relationships are complex, and simple. Love can show us many faces. During my cancer journey, I relied on my closest relationships for support. No one let me down.

After the Lovers comes the Chariot, associated with the astrological sign of Cancer. I don't think it is any accident that the Chariot can depict a rocky emotional ride. Indeed, love can be unpredictable too, however, the Chariot is controlled by a skilled driver. My cancer journey demanded the wisdom of all our archetypes in the tarot, daily, and during the most challenging of days, even hourly. The tarot is as fluid as our experiences. The Chariot speaks of a rocky ride, an unpredictable journey, but also a journey that has an end. During our challenging life experiences, it is wise to remember that all things pass, including our darkest days.

The next card in the Major Arcana is the Strength card, associated with the sign of Leo, which is ruled in astrology by the sun. We are reminded in the imagery of the tarot, which depicts a maiden with a lion, that Strength is not brute, but firm and gentle. We start every major experience in our lives with an opportunity to develop our strength, fortitude, and wisdom, providing we travel that road of experience with integrity, and a heart open for the learning. If we do this, we acquire new strength.

The Hermit card follows the Strength card and is another favorite of mine. The Hermit is associated with introspective Virgo in astrology. I have both Pluto (power) and Uranus (change), two very powerful planets in astrology, in Virgo. The Hermit is capable of great feats. The Hermit is capable of review, and of investigation and reflection, on what has occurred. The Hermit goes within, to examine and reflect on the detail of a challenge, to reach a destination. In the tarot the Hermit carries a lamp because the journey is long and dark. The Hermit carries a staff, and we know that he will find a way through that darkness. I read a quote, which I was particularly drawn to by Marcus Kantz, the co-director of the UK Tarot Association about the Hermit card. He reminds us that the Hermit is isolated and alone because he must navigate through the inner light of himself. I found during my cancer treatment that while my loved ones supported me, it was a road I had to travel by myself.

Following any experience in life, the Wheel of Fortune can turn in our favor, and to our disadvantage. The Wheel follows the Hermit in the Major Arcana. In astrology, it is associated with the expansiveness and benefits Jupiter bestows. The Wheel in the tarot placement is particularly meaningful for me. After the trials of the Hermit, and the introspection, and his guidance and strength, the Wheel of Fortune shows us that our situations can improve. However, were we faithful to the Hermit's strengths and what did we learn because after the Wheel of Fortune comes the balancing of the scales, the Justice card.

The Justice card depicts a queen holding both the scales of justice, and the sword of truth in her hands. It is associated with the astrological sign of Libra. Libra is all about the "we." Librans can see two sides and they demonstrate and represent balance. When Justice appears, it is always fair and embodies universal truth. We will either get back what we lost, or we won't and yet the lesson of Justice is that, ultimately, we get what is best for our spiritual evolution. In the early days of my cancer battle, I was confident that I would go back to the life I was living before. This could not have been further from the truth as I was altered physically through surgery. With radiation and chemotherapy, the legacy remains after treatment finishes and can impact for the rest of your life. Curative cancer treatment is harsh. I lost a lot of my social mobility, yet, with adaptation, I am living my best life. It is different from before, yet I cannot say that it is less fulfilling. Rather than living in the traditional, mundane society, I now live a very rich and purposeful spiritual existence. This blueprint event in my life was, perhaps in my karma, and, therefore, karmic justice was fulfilled because Justice, along with the Judgment (inevitability) cards, are two of the most karmic cards in the tarot deck.

Next, we have the Hanged Man which is associated in astrology with the sign of Pisces. It is a difficult image to look at for many. It depicts a man hanging upside down on a cross with a halo of light around his head. In the tarot, this card embodies suspension and the need to look at things in a different light.

It also speaks of sacrifice. The tarot is first and foremost a spiritual tool. When read correctly, we can see new horizons, and destinations, that arise from misfortune and tragedy.

The Death card — associated with the astrological sign of Scorpio — follows the Hanged Man and can also be uncomfortable for many. Yet, I see it as inspirational, because it represents the ending of old cycles and the beginning of new ones. If I apply that to my cancer experience, I realize that I look at my life in a different way now. I understand keenly the sacrifices that I have made to survive. The Death card illuminates the ending of one life, and the beginning of another for me. In my case, the beginning of my current work as a tarot reader, astrologer, and a spiritual teacher. I use the word teacher very sparingly. However, the skills and the gifts I've been given in this lifetime have been given for a reason. In fact, I completed a postgraduate diploma in education, and I did teach in adult education and in schools for a short time. Whatever workplace I was in, I always found myself in the job of training and mentoring staff. So here we see the blueprint of the cancer journey in action, and the development of my many spiritual platforms.

I am a Sagittarius sun sign and the next card after the Death card is Temperance which is associated with Sagittarius. In the tarot, the Temperance card features an angel with one foot on the earth, and one in the water and holding two cups, transferring water from one to the other. The sun is setting behind the mountains, and the road from the mountains leads to the water. The light of awareness is depicted by a halo around the angel's head, reminding us of the knowledge and wisdom gained through our journey, and that it leads to our goal of enlightenment. The Temperance card is all about healing, particularly healing of the emotions and the ego. Every critical experience in our lifetime, those watershed moments, require us to put the ego aside. In my cancer journey, I went from living largely an egoistic life, one in which career and educational achievements were a measure of success, and one where striving for the next goal was admirable. I wanted to be the best I could be in my career. Cancer leveled my ego. The Temperance card reminds us that extremes, no matter what the intention, are not healthy and balancing the emotions can bring forward healing and balance. The Temperance card is sometimes referred to as moderation. Cancer taught me to find the center and balance in all things, lest I forget.

I smile when I look at the tarot's Major Arcana because its creators were extremely clever. The next card after Temperance is the Devil card, associated with the sign of Capricorn and ruled by the task master Saturn. In most decks the devil has the two lovers chained to him. The Devil card can be interpreted as what chains you to the devil? Is it greed, is it addictions, is it habitual patterns that keep you in the dark night of the soul? Yet, behind the devil is the golden light of awareness. If we can only check ourselves and understand our weaknesses, we can turn those weaknesses into strengths. The silver lining in any cancer journey is the wisdom you gain along the way. You do this by having everything stripped away from you, as you fight the battle for your life. Every cancer warrior understands the lesson of the devil as we remind ourselves in that moment when we contemplate our mortality, of all the lost opportunities and the loop of negative patterns we allowed ourselves to repeat, and of failing to really understand what was important. Post-cancer, we understand and feel that golden light of awareness illuminating our journey through ignorance and temptation.

As I look back through my life, I see that I was given many intuitive warnings, often years before critical events occurred, yet I ignored them.

The next card in the tarot, the Tower, is associated with Scorpio and Aries (endings and beginnings) and the planet Mars in astrology. Mars drives forward lightning quick and often dramatic and volatile change. The Tower card breaks down existing structures, and rigidities, to reveal something new. In the tarot, the Tower is burning, and men and women are falling from its windows to the rocks below. The Tower reminds us that crisis can enter our lives when we least expect it. However, we should never be afraid of the Tower. Once our fixed beliefs that no longer serve us have been understood and changed, we can rebuild a structure that is far more beneficial and stronger. Although my life completely changed with cancer and its treatment, I have built something new, something softer, something healthier, and something far more real than what I had before. My new structure is underpinned with strong foundations.

I have had the same dream throughout my lifetime, two or three times. I get clairaudient words, along with an image of light, and the words hope, hope, hope. The word is uttered three times. In the tarot, the Star card (associated with the planet Uranus, change, and Aquarius — the idealist and humanitarian) reminds us that hope is not just an emotion, it is an intention and a belief. It is how we set and trim our sails and the destination we aim to reach. It is a navigator, and it finds a pathway forward through the illumination of intention and belief. I think one of the greatest gifts that cancer gave me was the knowledge that hope is real; that hope is alive, and that hope is available to us as a gift during our darkest passages.

The Moon card is associated with our moon and the sign of Pisces in astrology. In the tarot it depicts both the wolf and the domesticated dog. There is a large pond given the association with Pisces, a water sign, which represents the emotions. There is usually a crab emerging from the water. The moon and its light illuminates a path to the water and encourages us to look within to our feelings, and to what is hidden. Just as the sun in astrology is "I am," the moon is "I feel." The Moon card shows us that emotions, no matter how repressed demand expression. We can be both instinctive and wise in our emotional expression.

Cancer taught me tolerance and fortitude. It taught me patience. It tempered my fiery emotional nature because I realized that venting my emotions to the detriment of another or suppressing them was not healthy. Rather, tempered expression of emotions can lead to rewarding relationships with others, and with ourselves.

As much as the Moon is about our feelings, the Sun is about our actions. It is the great illuminator and lifeforce of the tarot. The Sun card follows the Moon and in the Rider Waite deck depicts a young child (the Fool) riding a horse. This child is full of happiness and joy, surrounded by sunflowers and the lifeforce and light of the sun. In astrology, this card is associated with the sun and the sign of Leo. The tarot is like the building blocks of life. Our lives can be harmonious and happy, and they can be full of the need to break out of old patterns that do not serve us and rob us of joy. The Sun card also reminds us to experience those moments of joy and happiness, just as we did in our childhood innocence. It reminds us that these moments and times can and should be experienced regardless of our circumstances, challenges, or events. During cancer treatment, I was able to find the most exquisite moments of joy because I was confronting my mortality. The thunderous electrical storm and the soft sunlight that emerged afterwards appeared as new to me because I was fully present in the moment. Even now, years later, I marvel at the beauty of nature and the simplicity of living daily because I am truly lucky to be alive.

Following the Sun is the Judgment card which is ruled by powerful Pluto and associated with the intense sign of Scorpio (transformations). The Judgment card speaks to the inevitability of endings, and the inevitability of change. Along with the Justice card, the Judgment card is another of the karmic cards in the tarot. It can often depict major karmic cycles ending. I have often quoted the saying that change is often desirable, frequently, necessary, and always inevitable. I am reminded of this every day. I take nothing for granted post-cancer. The Judgment card in its ultimate expression, speaks to us of the changes we will experience and endure during our lifetime. It is the second last card in the Major Arcana. The last card is the World card which is associated with Saturn in astrology. It too portends major endings of cycles as the Fool's journey ends. It speaks of the wisdom earned through all these experiences.

I realize why I now use the Major Arcana as a tool in my divination. It can be applied to every situation in our lives and, at the same time, can be reflective of our lifetimes and karmic cycles. As I shuffle the deck in my hands right now, as I am writing this, I understand that I can embody the Fool's energy one day, and the World card's the next. I also like to look at the tarot as a journey through our earthly experiences to reach wisdom, and to evolve and ascend spiritually. I enjoy the seeming randomness of the tarot. In drawing cards in random order, you can understand your experience. The card I draw today is the Empress, reminding me that I have the wisdom of experience to determine how I respond to those experiences in my life and that growth, not negative patterns are potential outcomes. That is the challenge of spiritual evolution. It is a product of many decisions; the wisdom to choose the correct path, born from facing life's critical events. At the base of the deck which reflects the underlying energies of any given situation is the Sun card, reminding me to create and savor happiness and joy.

Chapter 27

Survivor's Guilt

The problem with surviving was that you ended up
with the ghosts of everyone you'd ever left behind
riding on your shoulders.

Paolo Bacigalupi, *The Drowned Cities*

Survivor's guilt is commonly referred to as the experiences of
someone who survived a loss while others, or another, didn't.
Cancer wards are full of those who will survive, and those who
won't. From the beginning of my cancer experience, I knew
that I was reasonably early staged. We got to my cancer while
it was still encased in the colon because of two reasons: my
doctor had been hounding me to have a colonoscopy because
of symptoms and those symptoms were getting worse, and my
sister's diagnosis. Had I left testing any longer, I may not have
been so fortunate.

My surgeon told me upfront that he was going for "cured."
He insisted upon radiation and chemotherapy before the
surgery to shrink the tumor to give me the best chance for long-
term survival. Similarly, my oncologist wanted me to have mop-
up chemotherapy after surgery to maximize the chance that I
would remain cancer free in the future. At Stage 2a, and with
good pathology indicating the surgery had been successful, I
still chose the mop-up chemo. I didn't want to get down the
track only to find that the last lot of chemo would have picked
up any stray cancer cells left over from earlier treatment. My
elder sister Jane was diagnosed at a later stage. Just as she
had throughout my life, she went in front of me, and I learned
from her experience. What did I learn from her death? To be
honest with you, I'm still working that one out. You see, if I

had obtained my wish, we would be still sharing experiences, weekly and sometimes daily chats. The kind where you sit in your bathrobe in the morning and chinwag, and are still talking after your second cuppa, and, perhaps, glance at the clock on the wall only to realize it is late morning and your busy day likely won't start until after lunch. Ah, but the relaxed conversation reminds you that nothing is more important than the present company, and the familiar and homely vibe that calms your mood, and your worries, because you know for certain that if the earth fell through its axis, you'd have someone looking out for you, someone who wouldn't leave you behind. So, you see, I don't really know what I learned from her death and that's the classic pattern of survivor's guilt. There doesn't seem to be any reasonable explanation for why she didn't survive too. I'm not saying she wouldn't have wanted me to survive, she absolutely did because we were the closest of sisters and we wished each other the best in life. There was no doubt about that; you don't doubt bedrock love.

I understand the "survivor's" part well. I go on with my life, without my sister in it and that is part of losing someone close and the grief. I'm less able to articulate the "guilt" part. It is a feeling that words can't adequately convey. It's the images of her valiant attempts to stay alive, having surgery after surgery; it's her unwavering support of my journey and celebrating with me when I returned good test results. It's seeing her suffer unspeakable physical pain and being strong enough to carry it with dignity, and it's the look on her face when she realized hope was gone when the medical and oncology experts told her that. It's the part of me that didn't know what to say then, or where to look. It's that feeling of boundless shock that I drowned in, not knowing if this was real. She was to pass away and go, and I was to stay and live. Two sisters with the same cancer, in the same place, and one had to go in front. One died and one lived.

For months, years afterwards all I could rationalize was that she was eight years older than me, so being younger was a rationalization to live a little longer, as pathetic as that sounds. And I had looked after her, along with my other sisters when she was recovering from her many surgeries. I recall going for the jugular of a cancer survivor on an online support group, who, when I let the group know, she'd passed away, said: "Yes, I remember Jane, she kept backing up for those surgeries didn't she."

I replied, "The reason she did that was because her type of tumor was resistant to chemo. She had no other option but surgery, after surgery, after surgery if she wanted to live."

Another member of the group, a young mum who was diagnosed just after she'd given birth to a baby girl, intervened in her gentle way. "I'm so sorry you've lost your sister. She fought with such courage." (This brave young mum also passed away a few short years after my sister.)

Courage. Jane quietly carried her pain, and a dogged hope right to the end. She didn't want to go and was never ready to go. She even agreed to try a different chemo that might prolong her life despite the risks. She knew it may not work, however, when she was told no more surgeries were possible, there was no other choice left but to try one last lifeline, albeit a temporary one. I was with her that day; they couldn't find a vein at her first infusion because she was skin and bone. They sent her for a port — a device implanted under the skin in the chest region which is plumbed directly into an artery to make chemo infusion possible. Unfortunately, the surgeon punctured her lung when putting the port in because there was very little fat left between her skin and her lungs. It took weeks for her lung to inflate, and she was told afterwards that even high-risk maintenance chemo would not work. I was with her visiting at the hospital during those days too. Inevitably they told her, "Go home and set your affairs in order." Her six-year fight to live was over.

Yes, I was there through all that. When she couldn't stop shaking because death was unavoidable. When she told me that she would miss me when she died.

"You won't be far way," I said. "And I'm a psychic… I'll find a way to talk to you, so you won't miss me."

Those of us who have lost loved ones know that in the first few years after the loss, it is difficult to break through grief. It's encompassing and can be like sitting at the bottom of a dark well. I believe this makes communication hard for our loved one in Spirit. I have felt her around me a few times, not as many as I had hoped. Once I felt her presence acknowledging the love between us. On another occasion I woke with the feeling I'd spent time with her, that kindred, affirming, sisterly feeling I missed so much. I've also met her in the dreamscape on more than one occasion, yet it is not the same as sharing our lifetime together. I hope now that I've finally finished this book that it eases my grief and loss, though I suspect that after four years (as I write this), these feelings will be with me until I too pass into Spirit.

I hope that I can better understand my survivor's guilt in time, that awareness and insight will be the balm for that boundless shock that I still feel when I remember all that has happened because of our cancers.

She was right, as usual. In that phrase, "I will miss you," was the premonition of things to come. As much as she might miss me, I miss her most days of my life. The memory of my sister never dims. A lifetime of friendship is a precious thing to recall, still.

Chapter 28

Signs of Spring

We say that flowers return every spring, but that is a lie. It is true that the world is renewed. It is also true that that renewal comes at a price, for even if the flower grows from an ancient vine, the flowers of spring are themselves new to the world, untried and untested.

The flower that wilted last year is gone. Petals once fallen are fallen forever. Flowers do not return in the spring, rather they are replaced. It is in this difference between returned and replaced that the price of renewal is paid.

And as it is for spring flowers, so it is for us.
Daniel Abraham, *The Price of Spring*

I always knew I had to complete this story. I tried over seven years but couldn't quite do it despite writing professionally for most of my adult life. I just didn't have it in me because of the memories associated with both physical and mental pain of my own treatment. The grief was still too raw for the loss of my brave sister Jane. Sometimes, I would feel physically ill when I typed — so I put it all away, in a cupboard and shut the doors — firmly.

I can't remember a time in my life when I wasn't writing. My childhood adventure books written in my school exercise book, my adolescent poems, my creative writing and journalism at university, my 15 years as a newspaper journalist and editor; then there was my copious and productive writing for government and my national communication strategies for business, not-for-profits and government. Not to write at all through these post-cancer years has been foreign. It feels good now as I type the last chapters of this book. It's a testament to åll cancer warriors, the ones who survived and the ones who lost their valiant fight to live.

Life now is not how I envisaged it would be when I finished treatment. After being consumed with only the battle, I had to raise my gaze and survey the battlefield, each fight a scar on my physical body; each memory a reminder I had changed beyond recognition. Today, I live with the impacts of my treatment, but I am alive, nevertheless. I am part of this enduring tapestry not just of this lifetime but of the soul's evolution.

My cancer journey and my sister's story has been told. We are like you in your battles. There is an unspoken bond between you and me, and it is held together by our experience of suffering, of pain and of loss and grief. If you connect at all with our story, mine, yours, and my dear sister Jane's, then I do, indeed, go on and, with each connection and communication, the reason I survive is revealed.

On a good day, when I am feeling vital, I am reminded of the spring and of renewal. Life has always been about work for me, and I am still doing valued work. I know who I am, and what I am supposed to do, and that is a measure of success. I have purpose. Deep down in my soul, I know that I've journeyed far in this lifetime. I understand also that service to others, counts. As a result of my cancer battle, I connect with others in a universal and spiritual place that would not have been possible before. I am living my karma, learning, and evolving.

There is something more. I experience the joy of life in a way I hadn't before. It's a deep appreciation of living and loving, sensing the fragility of existence, with the inner certainty of meaning.

I love the simplicity of a clear and sunny morning, the soft light of a setting sun and the fullness of the evenings after the day, and I know that my guides and passed over loved ones are never far away. Most of all, I understand that all is as it is meant to be.

Part III

Channelings & Mediumship

Anyone who has physically incarnated on the Earth is energetically connected to the people they love, and to the Earth, indefinitely...

Jonni Gray, *Conduit: A Love Story Before, During, and After Life*

Channeling Nostradamus
(Herbal Healing)

I channeled the famous sixteenth-century French seer, physician, apothecary and astrologer, Nostradamus, on January 20, 2019, after a walk at a nearby golf course led me to a Rose Garden populated with the deepest of red/crimson flowers. I reached down and plucked a petal and rubbed it between my fingers. It left an oily residue. Around this time a man resembling Nostradamus came through, his facial outline and features imprinted on my third eye as I woke in the mornings. A fleeting view of him as I drifted off to sleep in the evenings. A knowing, that he had stepped forward and, importantly, had something to say. As I do with all my channelings, I let the energetic vibration of Nostradamus permeate over weeks, while I looked for signs and confirmations. The rose petal, as it turned out, was a valid sign that Nostradamus had given me, as you will read in the following transcript. This channeling was before the storming of the Congress on January 6, 2020, and the outbreak of the global Covid pandemic in 2020.

Hello, viewers. This is Maryann from Revealing Light Tarot. Today I want to tune into the energetic vibration of Nostradamus. The way that this channeling, if you want to call it that, this tuning in, this connecting clairvoyantly, even some would call it, remote viewing with the past, however you want to describe what it is, that gets you away from cliches and skepticism [when we use the word "channeling"]. We all can do this. It's just how much you have practiced, how much you are open to it, and whether your will is strong enough to connect.

Now, the way that Nostradamus came into my focus is through, I hate to say it, the rise of [former US President] Donald Trump. Of course, Nostradamus made what some see as a prediction about Donald Trump, and we'll ask him about that, toward the end of the reading.

When Donald Trump was elected, I innately felt that the world was entering into a very dangerous time. The events that would have occurred, from 2017–2020, would be extremely important for all of us.

Now, Nostradamus came into my frame more recently, a few weeks ago when one of my viewers asked me if it was true that Nostradamus predicted the end of the world in 2019. I don't dive into conspiracy theories, but we will ask, and we'll examine that in this video. More recently, I was going on my normal walk, which took me past a red rose bush, and I stopped. While I didn't want to pick the rose and disconnect it from its lifeline or life form, I did pluck a red petal out of that rose.

As I was walking back home, I ground the petal between my fingers and was quite surprised at the amount of water that came from it, or rose juice, that came out of that petal. I want you to just imagine or just leave that there as I move forward in the story. A couple of days ago, he came more strongly into my psychic medium vision. Last night I did a meditation where I connected with his energetic vibration. He took me to his home in the sixteenth century and walked with me to the back of his house.

We began to talk as we were walking, and I asked Nostradamus what he essentially wanted to bring forward. He showed me a bowl of red. It was like a reddish-tinged bowl of water. Now, I certainly didn't know about Nostradamus's work with herbs and healing herbs. I got on the internet then after I had that vision, and after I established that yes, he did want to speak and come through.

I immediately typed in red-colored herbal water and red-colored water/Nostradamus. Of course, what I was picking up on was his work with rose petals. Nostradamus trained as a medical doctor. He worked extensively with those with the plague, which was ravaging Europe at the time. Nostradamus was a French doctor. I think he was born in Saint-Rémy's or Saint-Rémy.

He worked with suffering families: children suffering with the plague. He brought forward alternative treatments which were quite successful. He made a mixture of rose water where he would grind the rose petals and he would make a concoction or a mixture of other healing herbs and substances. He would give this to the people who were suffering from the plague. Those who were not seriously ill recovered. He developed a reputation of being able to heal the sick.

He moved away from traditional type medicine towards astrology. When he was writing his predictions, he would meditate sometimes for quite long periods over a bowl of water with herbs in it. He was able then to bring forward predictions that we now see today, some of which have come true. I'm giving you that backstory for a couple of reasons.

At the time that I picked that rose petal, I had no idea that I would be tuning into Nostradamus's work. I didn't know about his work with herbs. I just knew him as an astrologer and someone who made these predictions. The clairvoyant image that I got of the reddish-tinged bowl of water was quite interesting because the words around that were that the herbs were so effective because in that form, in that water form, they could go straight into the body.

I think he made a concoction which would go underneath the tongue and be absorbed. There were herbal tinctures, herbal teas, herbal waters, brewing herbs, and a whole message there around the rapid way that herbs are absorbed into the body and can heal certain illnesses. Of course, if anyone's watching this that does have medical problems, you obviously know that you must first consult with those that are providing treatment for you.

However, things like herbal teas can be a good adjunct. You might want to talk to your doctors about that as well; how herbs might enhance or help, along with your orthodox treatment. That disclaimer aside, let's tune into Nostradamus's energy here. He did come forward at the beginning of the reading very strongly. Okay. He's turning up here and he has, what I would consider sixteenth-century head gear on, but it's also got a veil over it as well. He's a lot shorter than I thought he would be. I did notice this last night. I don't know what I expected. I expected him to be very tall. He comes forward a little bit differently to what I imagined him to be.

He's showing me some kind of text or something that he wrote in, and it's quite illuminated. He's showing me also an image of colors merging. I'm gathering this was when he meditated. I'm just getting, if you drop colors into a bowl of water, they start to merge and blend. I feel that his meditations tapped into a creative area, much like the artist might paint a scene, which is quite relevant to today.

I feel that he was tapping into a creative pathway, and he was also obviously clairvoyant. I feel that the way he used colors, he was quite aware of them. He used color, in some way, as a pathway. I'm getting the image of a compass here to guide him through a projection which enabled him to connect with the future. He also merged this with his writing. If you look at his quatrains, they are almost like poetry. He, again, through the artistic methods or artistic ways of tuning into, other dimensions, he was able then to project toward the future.

Now, I did ask him this morning if he would guide me in the questions that I'm going to ask him. I was going to put different questions together. When I sat down today, I came up with different questions to what I'd anticipated. They were very deliberately crafted, I think, with his influence.

I'm going to get started and just tune in remotely or clairvoyantly to him and go back to his backyard, or the area behind his home, and we sit down. There are a lot of rock formations where we sit at a table and sit on rocks, much like a table and chairs and outdoor setting. He's being very polite.

He's offering me refreshments. He's also making the distinction between his real name and the name that he's known by now.

He was born Michel de Nostradame. He came into this life in the sixteenth century. He then became Michel Nostradamus and now he's known as Nostradamus, but he's also talking about the importance of his early family, and his father as well. The influences of his family on him. Again, I'm asking him why he came here to me and he's showing me again this bowl, and in it is this water and a light within that bowl.

He came here to show people that the future was possible — that he could break the bounds of the present time that he was living in and bring forward treatments and healings, and predictions. He was here to show people there was so much more than their immediate environment. He is showing me that this lesson is particularly relevant today. That people, again, need to understand that there is so much more than their immediate environment, that it is possible to tune in or to connect with, or visit, other dimensions and that there is so much more that we don't know, because we've shut ourselves off from traditional healing.

He's saying that if he was able to accomplish that in the sixteenth century, surely with everything that we know, we should be more open, or we should be able to experiment more with what we've got now, given the knowledge between then and now. Okay, so that was his purpose, or that was why he was here. I'm asking him what he discovered. He's saying that time is eternal. He is talking about eternity.

I'm getting this image of something shooting right into the future, that we can move forward in time. He's asking me to follow a light, almost like the guide. What is the light? He's saying that your own spirit or your own energy, your own soul can easily travel into the future. The problem is in knowing what you see and then being able to express it.

That you may get glimpses of the future, but it's difficult for you to understand that's what they are, and to believe in them, and to trust them. Then, lastly to express them. That requires practice. He is also talking about the God Source and Spirit, that spark that takes you into the future is part of the God Source. I'm going to pull some cards now. I'm going to ask him how he did his predictions.

I'm going to ask him what he loved the most. Then I'm going to ask him, "what lessons do we need to learn in 2019?" Also, did he predict Trump and his downfall? Is that prediction, correct? Anything else in relation to 2019 or anything else generally?

With his energy, it is both big and humble at the same time. I got this image of him being a lot smaller than what I thought. Yet there is a quite a power to him. It was that power that allowed him to break boundaries in the sixteenth century. According to his biography, when he started to heal people, he got shunned and avoided as being like a witch or working black magic. That was okay.

He was strong enough and his early family life also helped ground him. There was just something about him that because he was considered a physician, that he was allowed, in some way, to explore the greatness of knowledge. Rather than being associated with a cult, he was seen eventually as being someone of quite a strong intellect, and they left him alone rather than take him off and throw him into the river with a rock tied to him.

He's saying that because he was male, he was less vulnerable because he's giving me those images of the witch, witches or, females who practice or healed with herbs weren't as lucky as he was. Apothecary is what he did. All right, let's ask, I'm going to go back to that bowl of water or rose water, or the rose petals. I'm feeling that he used a lot of that, this reddish-tinged fluid.

What did he discover about the healing properties of herbs? Nostradamus. Okay, so, he's talking about it; it's interesting. I'm using my Druid tarot deck, simply because it seems to fit the timeframe a little bit better. The Four of Cups and it depicts someone who is disappointed. There are lost opportunities but there is always something hidden no matter what the circumstances. I'm getting that he did work with plague victims when all was lost. There was something else that could help. He's saying that was a very strong lesson for everyone around him. In this deck there is the forest and I'm getting a real pull to the flowers around that cup.

He's saying that searching for that which remained hidden, and particularly when you are challenged by inaction or a stalemate, by the hardest of circumstances where nothing appears to be going forward. I'm getting strongly drawn to the red petals in this card. If only that person depicted in the card, who is looking away, could see what is being offered. He's saying that we need to be able to see more, see more than what's around us.

We need to know that there are potentially so many other ways of doing things. He's talking about loss here. He's talking about the number of deaths here which I feel weighed very strongly on him. We might cover a few of my questions at the same time because I asked what he loved the most. I'm getting that he loved his family, his home and his children, and his wife, and they were lost to him.

His reactions to that loss also helped his work when he saw other families losing loved ones and dying from a plague. He felt rather than just do nothing and accept one's fate, that if we looked hard enough around the environment, we could find the things that could assist us using the knowledge that we each have. The High Priestess tarot card is speaking of the type of knowledge that resides in all of us, and where the kind of wisdom that he accessed comes from; he accessed it from his subconscious.

Nostradamus had both a very strong conscious, analytical mind but also understood the power of the realm of the subconscious. The subconscious is coming forward to me, as if you open a door to another realm. He's saying that the subconscious was the doorway to that other realm. He sourced information from that other realm.

Now, the Seven of Pentacles card. He's talking about harvesting. He's saying that re-evaluation is needed when things are stuck, and he's talking about discovery. What did he discover? He discovered so much in the natural world that is there to assist us. Now, why wouldn't we be harvesting that? Now he's talking about the 10 of Pentacles. He's talking about the family.

Again, he's coming back to how important his family were to him, both his original family, his father, his mother, his siblings, and his own family. He's saying: why wouldn't you harvest everything you can? Why wouldn't you discover more, go into the furthest reaches of any realm you can access, to assist and help your family? I'm getting very, very, very strongly that family were extremely important to Nostradamus.

Here he is, as the Hierophant. He's talking about spiritualism and daily spiritual practices. He's speaking about meditation, and I'm just going to the power of meditation to connect with that other realm. I'm just going to spray meditation mist here, which has lavender in it. I was also able to find my rose water as well. I'm just trying to put a little bit of that on my hands.

The environment around us. He's speaking about using the esoteric sciences, spiritualism, the metaphysical, as avenues or guideposts to take you forward. That's what he's really known for in his sixteenth-century incarnation. His greatest hope was to cut through those stagnant situations and provide people with new starts. He was very much a man that resonated with ordinary people and with families.

He's saying those that seek to heal, whether that's via orthodox medicine or other healing modalities, do have this connection to people. He's also talking about having the confidence, I think as well. When I look, I've got a photo of him.

It's one of the well-known ones and it's a very old photo of him, and he's in that hat, that I saw at the beginning of this reading. When he did appear to me, he also had spectacles on.

I'm not sure what that was about and if there were spectacles in the sixteenth century, but he was wearing them when he turned up. He was also wearing that veil.

He's talking to me here about having the confidence to juggle, to search, and go out on a limb. He's saying that it's not manipulation when you do that. It's simply allowing your will to take you there. It's about letting your will instruct you.

What did he discover in this life?

The Prince of Cups card — he's talking about the love that was behind what he offered to people. Again, this healing aspect. He is also talking about the gift. He's talking about the gift that he gave us, in allowing us to understand that someone from the sixteenth century could connect with our present time and with the future. That indeed was a gift that he gave us. The 10 of Swords card. He's also talking about how his predictions shouldn't be seen through rose-colored glasses.

He's talking about those predictions which were couched quite strongly in destruction, and I'm thinking of the Trump prediction where he talks about blood flowing from Trump's mouth. He's speaking here of the language that he used which was not always literal. That blood coming from Trump's mouth represents the barbed swords that he uses with his words. He is also showing me that when people dwell in this kind of house, downfall awaits them.

Now, what's underneath all of this is his home and how important his home was. This isn't unlike where he's taken me. It's a village and it's a wooden door, stone cottage, or a stone house. He's talking about the fellowship that the home brings and the importance of celebrating that. That was very important to him which was why he again wanted to work so closely with families.

We talked a little bit about what he discovered. We talked about what he loved the most, his family. He's also talking about predictions through this video. I'm going to go to what the learnings are for us in 2019. I'm going to ask him about his prediction of Trump.

Okay, let's have a look. What do we need to learn? What are our biggest learnings currently, shall we say in 2019? The biggest — what I'm getting here is an image of a crucifix and from the crucifix a man walks forward basically.

What he's saying is that at this point in time, that kind of Evangelical Christian fire and brimstone warnings were designed to create fear and we need to understand that the real church is within ourselves. He's really encouraging us to step outside of the bounds of our existing beliefs and understand that so much more is possible for the human mind when we understand — in the subconscious realm that's available to us to use — to discover and to gain more knowledge, and if we want to travel to the future.

What are the lessons we need to learn in 2019? He's also apologizing for the hardness of the words that he used. I'm getting drawn to the colors, the merging of colors and red was so important to him. He used those colors to describe things for us which we now interpret as red blood, for example, but could have meant the violence of someone's words.

What are the lessons we must learn? This is the Empress card here and the abundance of what is within. I'm getting drawn to the heart chakra, the green chakra in the middle of this person's chest, and to understand that we can travel much further than our physical bodies. This is also passing on what we learned to our children as well so, that it can ensure the continuity of the knowledge and that the spiritual practices are passed down.

The challenge for us is when we don't connect, or we don't understand that the abundance lives within us. The heart chakra is the focus of the reading, so that's very important to him.

The Ace of Cups card here speaks of love and, again, I come back to his family and how important his love for his family was. He says love flows like a river. If you pour love into something it will be like the river; on a journey of its own. It will go forward, and it will end up in places that you cannot see yet.

He is speaking of victory and success, the Six of Wands. This card is signifying to me that it is calling to our soul family: those we have met in our various lives and connecting with the wisdom of our ancestors. It's putting that call out and understanding that we can access that in the subconscious realm.

Now he's speaking of transformation, beyond the physical body. We can connect with the spiritual realms through love, through our passed over loved ones, through our ancestral lines and through putting that call out.

He's speaking again of meditation. When you do, make sure that the environment around you is conducive to meditation. He's talking about the water and about tapping into the energetic vibration of water. He's saying that was important in his meditations which led him to predict the future. He's talking about understanding that we are supported by spirit even in the darkest of times and that he had a confidence in the non-physical realms that really transcended everything that the sixteenth century threw at him.

The Six of Pentacles card represents the giving and the receiving of help. Those that we do help come back to us in ways that we don't really understand. He's talking about the giving and the receiving that is the flow of this present life as much as it may influence our future incarnations.

He's speaking about the solar plexus chakra. Of course, that is the seat of our wisdom and our awareness. This is the image that I got around his predictions. He's talking about his intuition and he's saying that intuition alone is not good enough. You must have wisdom and awareness to be open to learning and its importance.

What is hidden from our view? He speaks of the earthly realm and of conflict and defeat. The Five of Swords in the Tarot. He's speaking about the need to develop wisdom here. Wisdom can help you manage these situations. Wisdom and awareness and knowledge can help you manage conflict and defeat.

I'm going to ask him one more question because I know it's the question that you all want to know. What predictions would he like to bring forward for Donald Trump? What do we need to know? Now, I'm going to read you the Quatrain relevant to Donald Trump's election in 2016:

The great shameless, audacious bawler.
He will be elected governor of the army:
The boldness of his contention.
The bridge broken, the city faint from fear.

And perhaps to his claims in 2016 and, particularly, in 2020 the election was rigged which led to his call for protests on January 6, 2021, which resulted in the storming of the US Congress:

The false message about the rigged election to run
    through the city,
stopping the broken pact; the voices brought chapel
    stained with blood.
The empire contracted to another one.

There is one other quote I will mention here that may refer to the assassination of Donald Trump. I don't read it that way. Let me find it as he talks about blood coming from Trump's mouth.

The trumpet shakes with great discord.
An agreement broken: lifting the face to heaven:
the bloody mouth will swim with blood;
the face anointed with milk and honey lies on the ground.

Nostradamus is speaking of loss, manipulation; loss and juggling in relation to Trump. The focus of the reading is the Death card. It's very difficult to know if he's predicting the end of his presidency or something else. Let's keep going. We're talking about the loss. He's predicting loss here. Loss for Trump. He's talking about the past, the Six of Cups card, union with the past, union with innocence. Reunions with more stable times.

He's talking about moving on from Trump. He's speaking about the nature of Trump, the *audacious bawler*, and he's talking about more benign influences and leadership emerging post-Trump. He is talking about women as well coming forward here, that the power of women is rising in this time. He's talking about the celebrations here, re-unions with the family, and he's talking about families being threatened by Donald Trump.

He's speaking about the illumination that will come from this time, and of new starts. Now, what is hidden from us, of course, this Queen of Cups cards. She so often comes forward when we're talking about Donald Trump. I'm feeling that a woman will bring forward information that will be instrumental in his leaving. I'm going to ask if Trump will be assassinated because of that Death card.

Or if he's not assassinated, potentially a health problem. The situation is so precarious. Will Trump be assassinated?

He is speaking about law enforcement, and burdens. He is speaking about the deals that potentially have been made. It's interesting, some sort of offer here. We've got giving and receiving help. What's hidden from our view is retreat, wounded, someone being wounded after battle. One more card disappointment.

Now, I just want to connect back into Trump's energy. It's so disconcerting. Nostradamus is here holding a book. Now he's a scholar and he has got his hands on several books, and he's talking about studying. Now, he's going to go back [to the Afterlife]. He's a learned man.

He's continually studying and he's studying to bring forward knowledge all the time. He's hoping that if we took nothing else from this video, we should understand the power of our unconscious mind and of that realm to take us, as explorers, into other places, other dimensions, to bring forward knowledge, and bring back knowledge. If we got that message in this video, then we will have learnt something, but he's also talking about the heart as well, the heart's ability to illuminate.

It's about your intention for seeking knowledge and the intention would be helping yourself, but it is essentially to help others.

Thank you. All right. This is quite a long video at nearly an hour, I'll leave it there. Thank you for tuning in viewers. It's time for me to stop now. Thank you.

Channeling Dr. Sigmund Freud
(Childhood Patterns)

The bearded and bespectacled face of Dr. Sigmund Freud came to me over the first few months of 2021. Dr. Freud was a very famous Austrian neurologist [1856–1939] and known as the founder of psychoanalysis. As with all my channelings, I let the images, messages and purpose of the contact permeate over time. In this way, I satisfied myself that this was a mediumistic contact and that I was allowed, compelled even, to bring Dr. Freud forward for my viewers. I believe mental health is aligned with physical health in ways we've yet to comprehend, and that is why I have included this channeling of Dr. Freud here.

It proved a challenging channeling as I found myself being psychoanalyzed, which was slightly uncomfortable for me. In any case, the following is the record of this channeling on April 12, 2021.

I've been wanting to do a channeling now for quite some time. I've been wanting to channel Dr. Sigmund Freud. Now, I don't know why Freud has come through so strongly, but he's telling me I do know, and that's very consistent with his work. Obviously, in my university studies, we have touched on Freud. The thing that I remember most about Freud is the id [instinctive, impulsive part of the mind] and the ego [the part of the mind responsible for a sense of self/personal identity].

I always felt that Freud was way too earthly anchored, if you like, even though he is considered the father of modern-day psychoanalysis. He is here now and he's quite agile, and mentally agile. As I talk, I'm hearing him respond. I've noted down some questions here and we'll work through them. I hope they're the right questions. Let me just describe his energy to you.

At first, I got him very late in life when he was quite physically comfortable because I'm getting the word "austere," that he was quite austere. Very obviously, piercingly intelligent, but very rigid and very serious. Of course, one of my questions is: "Any regrets?" He's telling me that dining at the table, sampling the delights of life, he should have done more of that. I think that's why I got him later in life because he was so much more comfortable then to what he was [in his earlier life].

The seriousness with which he approached his work, he was discovering [more and more], and he was really motivated to push through. That is why he's a pioneer. That's why he's a trailblazer, because he pushed through and he discovered the unconscious and what happens when we repress the unconscious, and how that develops into neurosis later in life, but that's not why he's come forward to me. He's wanted to come forward now for a few weeks, but it always needs to be the right time with these channelings. Today was the right time, it appears.

There's a certain amount of stillness that you need to listen to and hear. The reason that he wanted to come forward with me is that he feels the connection, and the importance and the exploratory nature of spiritualism. He didn't get that in his lifetime with what he discovered. When he looked at the unconscious, he did see it as a vast reservoir. I'm really getting this word "reservoir" very strongly. He thought that the reservoir was contained within this body. He only thought in terms of one lifetime.

What he wants to bring forward is that he now knows that what he discovered, the unconscious, is vast. It's virtually untappable. It goes right back to infinity and then forward and back. Nobody would be able to tap into its entirety. While he was able to get to what motivated people in this lifetime in terms of their unconscious, he couldn't make that link between past lives and how they might affect [the current lifetime], and reincarnation, karma, and the blueprints that we come into this life with.

I'm going to ask him if there is such a thing as destiny and fate. He brings me to the will, the spiritual will, and how strong that will is determines how much progress we make, so that if someone is aware spiritually, they're more likely to examine the lessons and learn from the lessons so that they don't have to repeat them. This vast reservoir, I want to go back to, as I said, the father of modern-day psychoanalysis, able to do wonderful work with people to solve, to fix, to heal neurosis.

I want to go back to that and why he has thought it is so important to come through on this point today. He's saying take sexuality, for example. He was quite, I won't say fixated, but some *would* say fixated on sexuality. He is asking me to go back to my childhood and discover where [and when] I got so critical. He's saying that's a self-defense mechanism. [laughs] This is very difficult [for me].

Okay, so sexuality. Take sexuality, for example. Someone that comes into this lifetime with a mixed or a dual sexuality could very well be learning how to balance, learning how to express, learning to be authentic, for example. Now, he would've traced that back to childhood. A mother complex or a father complex. I want to get to the mother in a minute. In fact, what he was missing was what happened before this current lifetime.

He's sort of alternating between those kinds of ideas and then slipping back into psychoanalysis as well. Both are equally valid in allowing someone to understand why they're experiencing the things that they are; why they're experiencing mental health challenges or mental illness. Again, that's a choice when they come in. It's part of their blueprint. Something around the complexity of mental illness is a particular challenge that people choose before they come into this lifetime.

He's just reassuring me that we are all safe; that we are protected because the complexity of mental illness is such that even trying to understand something that you can't... If you look at neurosis, it brings forward a lot of anxiety. That message around safety that we did choose that and, ultimately, it doesn't matter how tough and how dark, and how bleak things get. The light is always there, and the lesson is always there, and the help is always there.

When I first opened up for this reading up, I got the image of the mother.

I feel that Sigmund's mother was very important to him. I feel that he's telling me that she was his everything because the mother is a way of anchoring. He also faced his own mental health demons and challenges. Part of working through those was to help others. While he was working through that with other people, he was coming to understanding himself. He's telling me that's a little bit of what I do with my spiritual work; that I go, and I explore. I try to find the answers and those answers can often be found in other people.

He's tipping his hat to Dr. Carl Jung, who was a student of his who looked at universal consciousness. He's tipping his hat because he took it a little bit further, but I'm still getting not far enough because the gap here at this point in time for "orthodox" medical practitioners, psychiatrists, is to connect the dots with what is occurring with the patient and factor in [a spiritual factor] with everything else, everything else that's happened in this lifetime, and to take it a little bit further and look at the spiritual aspect of what is occurring. Because when those connections are made, the discoveries can be stronger. The discoveries for the patient can be stronger.

I'm getting his focus on instinct. I've just got a picture up of him. I don't know why I chose this picture. It's him when he's older, a lot older, and I feel that he was less rigid. I wouldn't call him uptight, but there was an element of that to him. He's just saying that when we're rigid like that, it is a way of managing anxiety or managing the internal tumultuousness in us. Then we hold ourselves quite rigidly.

Again, if we were to let go of that rigidity, it will make us more comfortable. Rigidity won't protect from those feelings of fear. In fact, the best chance of managing that is to soften and let go. Let go and lean into it, rather than resist it. Sexuality, the id, the instincts. I feel he was very, very, very good, very piercingly good at picking those instincts up in people.

He was, without a doubt, a brilliant mind, a far-seeing mind. He could see right into the personality, right into the id, right into the ego, and what he termed the super-ego. Again, there was a fourth dimension. He keeps wanting me to repeat this, that his work didn't go far enough. Connecting with the spirit. Why are people connecting with the spirit? Because they know innately that we haven't gone far enough.

This is almost like another frontier. The exploration of this frontier is occurring now in this time, in this place. It's very critical. He's telling me it's a critical time where we're moving away from what we can see, toward finding and looking for the things that we can't see, because we instinctively know that they're there, that the things that we can't see, we know are there. We just have to find them.

It is in the instincts to search, to explore, to want to move beyond instinctive behavior. What we're seeing now is instinctive behavior across the world in our leaders. We're seeing this and returning to instinctive behavior and moving through things like ego. I'm coming back to the instinct. We're seeing an illness there, in operating purely from the instincts. He's saying it's quite sad that that is all these people are willing to engage with.

He's saying that if you think about a spectrum, you've got the instinctive behavior here, and then you've got the spiritual or the higher plane, the higher behavior, the higher motivations, which go beyond just values and ideals that you learn in childhood because that was his definition of the super-ego. He's going to a knowing. It's a knowing of that reservoir that I spoke about — and I come back to that word "reservoir" and why he wanted to come through.

It's a knowing that the reservoir is there, and it is so infinite. It's a feeling. We just know it's there. It's natural to want to explore that and so that's what we're moving into now.

What more could he have done? I'm going to his dream work. He didn't understand at the time. He focused on the emotions that were generated during the dream. He used that in a way, this psychoanalysis, rather than accepting the possibility that the dream state was connected to this vastness.

He's saying, in some ways, his work was limited. The unconscious doesn't just go down. It goes up. It goes sideways. It goes everywhere. That's important. He's telling me that he saw the unconscious as being embedded and going down almost into these instinctive sexual motivations, but the unconscious doesn't do that. It goes up. It goes to the exploration. It goes back and forth between that vast reservoir.

I asked if his work was complete.

If he had started to do that, he could have at least then looked at this concept of time even in one lifetime. He could have perhaps projected forward almost like a prediction, which then would have influenced his work. That's what he would've liked to have done even just in his lifetime, is to go forward in a patient's lifetime, to look at the growth and development if the lessons are learned, and then look at the projected growth and development if they're not learned.

Then once that is established, then to start incorporating a very gentle spiritual aspect to his work, that's what he would've liked to have done.

What was he trying to accomplish? He was trying to accomplish accessing the hidden, what was hidden, that he assumed, was in the lower planes. That was quite valid because we still work that way now, but there's more. I'm going to pull some [tarot] cards now. He had a tendency in this lifetime to be very hard on himself. I'm coming back to the mother. The mother figure in his life.

I don't know. I haven't read around his relationship with his mother. I'm sure it's there. I'll go back after this reading because it's something that was brought through that's relevant. It was a matter of wanting to live up to his mother's image of him in some way. He was quite hard on himself as a result. I'm not sure that I want to go this deep, but there were elements of his mother that were incorporated in his personality. He was wanting to solve that mystery as well.

Okay, all right. The things in his mother that caused him the most problems, he realized were in himself. He wanted to find the answers for that. Going back into the childhood and understanding that the patterning was also part of what he wanted to discover about himself.

I want to ask what sort of information he wants to bring through. I'm going to colors. I don't know why I'm going to colors, but I am. Everything in this world is color. Some of the color therapists have done quite good work with color emotion choices. The energy vibration of color is where I want to go. He's telling me this is probably more suited to a Dr. Carl Jung channeling here because Dr. Carl Jung worked a lot with archetypes.

Something around color. Color can be predictive. Color choices and predictions. Predictive as in where the patient is at or up to, and that our attraction toward colors can tell us a lot about ourselves. Everything is color. Everything is light. Everything is color and everything is light. I asked what [tarot] deck he wanted to use. I've pulled the Spellcaster's deck because he's showing me that so much of the work back in the time that he lived dealt only with a society that wasn't inclusive.

The Spellcaster's deck includes archetypes and imagery from all races, or not all, but other races across the world. All right. He's psychoanalyzing me as we speak. He's talking to me about guilt and not having to carry the guilt of others on my shoulders because I feel guilty on their behalf. That's really to do with other things within me. I just want to say, "Get out of my head a bit." [laughs]

He's saying, "You asked me in, and so you're getting the benefit of that." Psychoanalysis can be difficult. It can dredge up a lot. He's telling me that once you dredge something up, you clear it. You clean it. You purify it. It's able to flow unimpeded again. That's the value of psychoanalysis. Again, letting go, not being rigid, and leaning into the lessons. Dr. Freud, what messages would you like me to bring through?

The King of Wands has come through quite strongly. That's interesting. The King of Wands is, again, standing in your own power, but being inspired to stand in your own power. The King of Wands is ready to lead a journey. He's telling me that everyone can be a leader in their own lifetime. Everyone has a story. Everyone has something to offer. Everyone can lead.

This competition that often comes into so many, or so much of the way that we live in this 3D existence, this competitiveness, really, is illusionary. Because if we realized that we're all leaders and we acted like leaders, then there would be no need for that competition. Part of leadership is listening. He's bringing forward the Justice card. Now, I'm getting, also, another hit that our leadership is wrong now; that it's out of balance.

I go back to the instinctiveness of our current leaders. There's a wheel in the background of this card. It's the Wheel of Destiny. We talked about destiny earlier on. There are certain points when these lessons are stronger and we're at a critical point. All right, the Nine of Swords. He's talking about anxiety. He's trying to soothe our anxiety now.

He's understanding that our leadership, the justice, the destiny, the karma that's occurring across the world now; the time that we live in, is a very anxious and worrying time. I'm sure there's a lesson here, a lesson for each of us in this larger picture. Strength and endurance are other important messages that he's bringing forward and taming the beast within. I'm feeling a big draw around instinctive behavior.

Basically, what he's bringing through, he's quite worried about, he wants to make this point. He's worried about this, that the instinctive behavior where people rush in, and they don't consider another, is going to provoke lessons here. We need to move beyond the instinctive and we need to have that connection with ourselves. It's almost like the self fighting against the self.

We now have the Queen of Wands. We have both the King and the Queen of Wands in this spread so far. The Queen of Wands is someone that does use intuition; that does use this spiritual connection, this, I guess, knowledge of something higher to act, and react, beyond an instinctive way of behaving. There are messages around the divine feminine here that are coming through. Justice is the challenge for our current leadership that operates only instinctively through the ego.

I'm pulling the Lovers card.

This is heart centered. This is the softening that I was talking about that's come through in my other readings. This is a reunion with self. This is directly connected to the rigidity that anxiety and worry provokes. Just as we miss things when we act instinctively, we will miss things when we are anxious, when we are worried, when we are rigidly protecting ourselves.

The Three of Pentacles. There's a strong message about working with others to fix something. It's like fixing humanity at this point in time, because it's careering off-track. It's regressing back to the instinctive, to the id and it's listening to the lower. It's not listening to the higher. There is a strong message here about reunions with self and reunions with … It's almost like family. The family of humanity. That needs to be fixed. There need to be those reunions. We've got the Star of Hope coming forward here. Again, hope needing to light the way.

When we see this contrast between this instinctive, the intolerant; racism is instinctive because it's straightaway a focus on what is different to you. We need to understand that we are bound together. We are bound together because we are part of the same source. Once we realize that, once we transcend the body and we can look at things in a spiritual light, we've got more chance of that reunion with self and reunion with a heart-centered approach.

The Ten of Pentacles, the monetary aspect. Again, an instinctive survival mode, wanting to accumulate more than what one needs.

The Three of Cups. He's asking how we support one another. Do we do that over a drink or many drinks? The way that the support is focused on the bodily aspect of things. I'm getting a real draw to the physical body, the instincts, and not engaging with that higher self.

Once we do that, once we engage with our higher selves, we can offer real, meaningful, and lasting support. We can dispel insecurities almost magically. It's like waving a magic wand. The insecurities that are causing people to act out or act up. It's interesting. What's hidden from our view is loss. Okay, so it's almost like we must lose ourselves to find ourselves, is what I'm feeling that he wants to say.

Okay, I just want to see if there's any final messages here that he wants to bring forward.

Has he said everything that he wanted to say? Okay, he's thanking me. He's calling me a kind lady. Okay, he's saying that that part of me is my higher self. The guilt and the regret, that's the lower self. He is saying, with some sort of irony, that if we were operating through our higher self, there'd be no need for psychoanalysis. Again, the mind is always drawn to learn, to discover, to explore, and all these things contribute to [our journey] home.

Okay, I'll leave that there. I just want to take a moment now to thank him for coming; thank him for coming forward. He's telling me that doing so was in his self-interest there that he did. He also wanted to connect with me for other reasons as well. Most of all, he's coming back to this idea of a vast reservoir and how important it is to navigate within your own vastness, including the possibility of other lives; the possibility of our own choices that we made before we come here, before we came into this lifetime.

If there were two choices that you could make to be happy or unhappy, if it came down to that, what would you choose? What would you choose? He said taking small steps to be happy is very healing. Okay, I'll go along with that. I'll agree with that. All right. Okay, he's telling me he might come back again at some point in the future. He says when we've learned to really choose this higher way of operating rather than this instinctive way of operating, he said there won't be a need, as I said, for people like him.

Okay, so where does it start? Again, it comes back to the mother. It comes back to the mother and the father, and incorporating the spiritual aspect into teaching children that are coming into this world. He said that will happen in time and that is part of the evolution of humanity as well. Don't despair in this blatant instinctiveness that you've seen from your leaders today. It's all part of a divine purpose to learn, to explore. It's us exploring our own divinity.

All right, thank you so much. All right, yes. Okay, he's leaving. All right. Sorry, but I'm feeling a sense of relief because there were many times during that channeling where I was copping a bit of psychoanalysis as well. Okay, so I'm going to do a couple of things now. I'm going to go back and have a look at his relationship with his mother because that was intriguing. I might also look at Carl Jung and whether he touched on the vastness of other lives and the spiritual connection, or I might find somebody that has melded the two.

For now, that was the channeling of Dr. Sigmund Freud. I'm grateful that his energetic vibration was present and that I was able to learn from it. I will review this video with that in mind, that I will learn from what came through today. Thank you very much for your support. As always, I hope you enjoyed this channeling and I'll be back again soon. Thank you.

Channeling Edgar Cayce
(The Sleeping Prophet)

I channeled Edgar Cayce, known as the sleeping prophet, on the February 17, 2020. Cayce was born in 1877 in Kentucky, USA. He was a healer, a mystic and clairvoyant. He would go into a trance-like state and bring forward information on healing, dreams, the afterlife, the future, and nutrition. I was to find out in this channeling his counsel on healing through nutrition, though I knew little about Cayce before the session. Of note, was the image of a light being crossing a "light bridge." Later, I was told that he had received information from such a "being." As with all my channelings, I look for the validation after my channeling sessions as indications I did connect with the energy of Cayce.

I'm going to do something this afternoon I wasn't intending on doing, but I'm being guided to do it anyway. I'm not really set up for it. I'm using my camera which I'm still unfamiliar with, but I'm getting the impression that I need to have faith and so I'm going to do this anyway. I have been asked in the past to channel Edgar Cayce. I felt his energy a couple of days ago come in.

I guess it was when I contemplated, whether I should channel him. The way that my channelings work is that someone comes to my mind. Sometimes that's by a request, sometimes it is out of the blue. It's a process where someone will come into my frame of reference, and then I see them, and I decide. I wait for the energy to build and start the channel. In this case, this was a little bit different for several reasons. People have requested that I do this channel.

It's a little bit of an intimidating channel. He was such a giant in his last life, in his earthly life. I'm feeling though that that's not a description that he's happy with because he still recalls this earthly existence. I feel that due to his background, he always carried with him some regrets. I asked him if he did have any regrets in his life. He talked about his attitude of not getting above your station in life. Even though he had a view which was really encompassing "to the edge of the universe and back," he was from humble beginnings and that, in a way, held him back in this earthly existence.

Even though he had the freedom of mind, he still had the judgments that other people put on us in relation to our early beginnings. The family that we come from, the amount of money that we've got, whether we need other people's help or whether we don't. This was a man whose higher consciousness was able to go literally to the edge of the universe and back, yet in this earthly life he was still limited by the circumstances that he was born into.

I've picked a photo of him. I don't know if you can see that. I haven't got a viewfinder here, but it's Edgar Cayce when he was a youngish man. When I first saw him, I thought there was an energy about him that was quite unsettling, particularly around his eyes. I do feel that this photo was taken at a stage where he was afraid of the gift that he'd been given. Perhaps not so much the gift, but other people's reactions to it, so he was unsure about how this would be accepted by society.

I did grow up hearing about Edgar Cayce. He was a little bit before my time. I had an old book on him that I don't think I ever got round to reading. Before I started this reading, I went on and I looked at his site, and had a brief browse around that site. I know that he was very focused on health and well-being and that, I think, was the clincher for me when I decided whether I would bring him through. I thought that I might have the opportunity to learn something.

I'm getting a real draw to the immune system with him now just while we're on the health and well-being before we get into the reading. This is around when your immune system is depleted. He's telling me that at different times in his life it was depleted simply because he couldn't afford good nutrition. I think at around the time that this photo was taken, that might have been one of those times. He's talking about nutrition being a big focus of his, simply because, back in his day, it wasn't as though he could go to the supermarket and buy fresh green organic vegetables. It wasn't like that at all.

The immune system is connected very much with your nutrition, and diet. When he did come through initially, I felt a great weight of heaviness come upon me. I tried to figure out what this might be. Almost like my body was made of stone and I do believe that is what I felt with him in the trans-state. Now that I'm really sitting in his energy, he's coming across much older and he has a lot of light behind him around his head area. I'm feeling that he had the gift of sight, as they say, and the gift of light.

There is a light in him that he had from a very early age, and when he closed his eyes and he shut out the world, that's when he could see something different. That's when he could see what the light allowed him to see. I do feel that, as I said, this heaviness for me is around him going into the trans-state. I'm just going to focus here for a minute, and we'll start with our first question because when I started to channel before, he did come through in his early life. I do feel again, I'm seeing a large family sitting at the table. There's a baby in a highchair and there are younger children sitting around.

He had a very high regard for women that began with his mother and then moved through, I feel, to his partnership in life, in marriage. There's something around this light that I feel that his mother might have had as well. I'm not sure what the story is, but I'm just seeing a baby in a highchair, in a larger family being touched around the head by the mother, and this light coming in. All right, let's have a look at what else he wants to bring forward. I'm just getting a real draw to his third eye and this light. It's almost like his head is made of light.

I feel that he may have had the assistance of a guide, or it's some sort of light being that came through to him when he went into trance, and it assisted him. I'm just seeing someone coming through a tunnel, a light being moving their way through, and there's a blinding light. I feel that when he went into trance, he was assisted by a particular being. A being of light. There's just something around this incredible light in his head or around his head area. That "being" showed him where to go because I'm getting the image of arrows, almost like a guide.

When he was in trance, he was able to connect with this guide. We'll just call it the "guide." This guide took him to places. As I said, as far out as the edge of the universe and back again and spanning across time. Travel in this light-filled space was not difficult for him. When did this start? I'm feeling that he feels this was very lucky. This gift was very lucky because I'm just seeing he's showing me a horseshoe now. Some of these images are going back to his early childhood so the time in which he was born, the era in which he lived.

He felt that this gift gave him luck and gave him an opportunity to strive forward in this life and to become known, although he was not necessarily seeking fame and fortune because I see him with a blindfold on which means that his focus was always on ... the importance was always on this light. When he closed his eyes, when he went into trance, that was where he felt he was lucky that he was able to see what he was able to see and do what he was able to do.

I'm getting the pull to around his early twenties, which was around the time that this photo was taken. He had anxiety around how his gift would be met by society, but he's also throwing a challenge out as well. I feel that was what he did. He threw a challenge out to society to, well, believe him or not. Of course, he was quite confident in that way because he was so often right. He was so often able to know the things that others would not know and that's simply because he was able to travel to wherever he wanted to go when he was in trance.

Why was he given this and what was his purpose in using this gift? What I'm seeing now are trees and new growth. I feel he was a prophet. He was known, of course, as the "sleeping prophet." He was here in a time that didn't accept the type of work that he did. He was here to allow for new growth in the Collective Consciousness, in people's souls. So, the soul journey, the soul's growth, was particularly important to him.

I feel that this is where the soul's growth was only as important as the heart as well. I feel that he put heart into his work because I'm just getting a draw to the heart chakra. His life's purpose was to show and demonstrate, provide an example, and encourage enlightenment so it was an evolutionary gift that he gave us and that was his purpose. It was all about evolution of the spirit.

All right, what did you learn in this life? I know that I've got several questions, and I'm trusting him to lead me to where I need to go.

He's giving me an image now of a boat, its movement, and its travel. It's also moving on. The ability to move on, to move forward. Movement is one of the things. The benefits of movement. Now, I don't know how often he moved in his life, and I don't know why he's showing me this boat, but I'm just getting that the image is transition. Transition from this life to the next. He learned about that in his lifetime. I don't know much about his writings or his prophecies, but there is an image given to me of someone transitioning.

What did he learn in life? He learned about moving forward, moving on, and transitioning. I don't even think it's between this life and the next. I don't even think it's that. I think it's movement generally, whether that's between lives or across the astral plane. It's movement that he learned about in this life.

Why did you work with people who were in ill health? Why did you diagnose illness because at one point, I think he was arrested because he was thought to be practicing medicine.

What was the interest? Look, I don't know about his childhood, but I feel that there was some kind of ... I don't know whether one leg was shorter than the other or he had some sort of limp or he got some sort of illness, but this is also tied up with the conditions of the time. He witnessed, he saw, or whether someone close to him, his brothers, or it could have been even his sister, there's some kind of ill health that he witnessed that was very close to him that set him on that path because so many people couldn't afford the things in those days, good nutrition, medical help. He looked for simplicity and the simple answers to help people.

The things that were in their control, the things that they could do, going right back to basics such as nutrition.

The central nervous system was very important because he was so sensitive. I feel when he was in these trance states, he was able to pick up or read, I'm getting a good pull to that one, he was able to read his own central nervous system. He's telling me that's correct. He was able to discern patterns, discern anomalies, discern where something needed to be fixed or needed some help or was out of whack, and then that allowed him to diagnose and then, of course, suggest treatments.

He wasn't a medical doctor. He wasn't professing to be a medical doctor, but he was able to read his own body. After he started to read his own body, he was able then to read other people's bodies. I'm feeling that the ability to move into trance and do this diagnostic work came about initially in dreams, so he didn't always start by just going into trance, I don't think. It came to him while he was in dreams and so he understood that the mechanism was some kind of sleep.

Of course, then after that, we had that relaxing and trance state. I am feeling this heaviness, like he left his body when he was doing this work. I could feel the heaviness of the body and the rising up of the astral body. Also, I feel that he was able to look down upon his own body as well and upon other people. He was privy to conversations. Again, this movement and this travel. He was privy to pretty much being able to go wherever he wanted to go and to hear and see anything he wanted to see, almost like he had a camera in any location.

I do understand, also, he was able to absorb knowledge. Again, there's something around the light here that he was able to absorb the knowledge within books and then use that knowledge. I feel that that was connected to light, to something around the speed of communication.

***

Sorry, my camera ran out of battery, and, of course, I'm restarting recording on my phone. I'm having faith that this channeling needs to be done, so I'm going to keep going with it.

When I was changing over my cameras, I did get a lot of clairvoyant images around the water, and particularly, plants within the water. I am guided to say that there are plants that live in water that can be found in lakes and ponds. I'm not so much feeling the sea, but there is a lot in this earth that can assist our health that we don't know about yet. There needs to be a revolution, that we need to go back to the earth, and establish that relationship with the earth so that we can get to know what the earth can offer us. It's almost as if everything that we need, if we live simply enough, is provided for us. I feel that that's not just a Shangri-La, that is achievable if we want it to be, on this earth right here and right now, but of course, everything is so complicated. Everything is so dense, and we operate in the dark in many ways. If only we were to use the light, use the light of consciousness I'm feeling, to discover and to travel, to move forward, then we could find things that are needed right in the here and now in relation to our health and well-being.

I will take that on board myself. That message came through, I feel, for a reason.

What do you want to bring forward currently for my viewers? What is critical at this stage of our evolution? I'm feeling there's something around when we sleep, and there's also something around relationships with each other. Around the connection that we all have when we're in that dream state, if we only knew how to move within that dream state, there would be a lot to discover.

I'm seeing the explorer here. It's as if this explorer has left the mine because I'm getting the image of a mine and walking out of the darkness and into the light, walking toward the light. I'm feeling that one of the main messages is to pay attention to your dreams, and to use your imagination and visualization whenever you can and bring that light through your body. It is very cleansing when you run that white light, or any type of light [or color], really ... when you run that energetically and visually through your body, it's quite a healing, cathartic process.

There's one simple thing that we can do, and in the dream space as well, is to set your intentions even before you go to sleep. Set your intentions, "I want to discover this. I want to explore that," and see where that dream state takes you. Start to use your dream state for discovery because it is a gift. It is a gift that we have. We don't necessarily understand what occurs within the brain when we are in that sleep state. We understand the science behind the REM and the various sleep disorders, the various sleep patterns, the way the scientists describe sleep, but they don't know really what occurs. I'm getting this image of the light. The light in the part of the brain that controls sleep is a portal and a doorway to spirit. Not the afterlife. It's not afterlife, but to life. We don't need to take the slow way; we can get a lift. We can get that vantage; we can learn to discover if we only unlock the key to movement in our mind. How do we do that? What is the key? That is sleep, and that is imagination, and that is visualization.

Learning to think in pictures, he is telling me, is a very powerful skill. There is one small step that you can take next time you're thinking — to start to see it in your mind's eye, to start to think in pictures and see where it takes you. What he's telling me is you're bound to discover something.

I'll pull some cards now. Mr. Cayce, what would you have liked in your life? He says he would have liked some formal education, to have come across like a professor. He would have liked to have done that, to learn more formally and to have those qualifications. That was not in his grasp due to his financial circumstances. He was reliant on other people, and almost performing in a way, a circus act, to get the money to do the work that he wanted to do.

What did he want to do? One of the most important things to him was to not just diagnose, but share this as well, the ability to scan the body in an altered state. In the astral state, the ability to scan your own body and make your own diagnosis, and then take action to repair something or fix something or address a problem. That's really what he wanted to do with his life, but he was held back by being, and I'm just getting the phrase, in the servitude of others. The servitude, so that tells me that he was in service in some way.

I'm getting a pull to a sister of his, and I don't know why she's so important. It was somebody that he was quite close to.

Let's have a look at the messages you want to bring through these cards, Mr. Cayce. What he's saying is that the collective consciousness is weighed down and very heavy at this moment from all the divisions and the fracturing. I'm feeling the fracturing. Fragmenting or fracturing. It's not cohesive and it's not whole, our consciousness, our collective, and it's pulling away. It's unhealthy, he's telling me. If I can scan it, what he's seeing is that there are parts that are pulled away from the whole. The whole can't function properly until the other parts are joined. It is the lesson of the collective to bring those that are isolated back in the fold. Those that are isolated — it is their lesson to understand the darkness that they sit within or that they are within. I'm getting this draw back to the light, the light of consciousness, the light of spirit, the light of God. I'm getting a draw back to that light and I am seeing that journey. The journey can be long and arduous. It's not guaranteed we will get to that destination. We've always got to do this traveling.

I'm getting he was a traveler. Not a time traveler, I don't think, but a traveler through landscapes, through the astral plane, through the collective consciousness, through the light. This "being" that walked with him, that showed him, that guided him, enabled all possibilities for him.

Of course, that was part of the work that he did, but at this time, in answer to the messages he wanted to bring through, it is around those that have broken away, coming back into the light.

That can be impossible sometimes, but it is around getting the vibration of the collective consciousness right. It's not as if some part must physically travel back. The vibration must be able to reach that which has disentangled itself or broken away. I'm seeing the collective consciousness as a living … I won't say organism. That's not the right word, but as a living energy, and it is damaged now. It's damaged because we haven't stopped to repair. We've been careless.

Even the worst of authoritarian leaders or dictators are a part of the collective, and again, when that vibration changes, then they would not be able to do what they are doing now, whether that is invade a country or start a war. The collective has a role in changing that vibration. The collective isn't powerless.

Everything is movement, everything is energy, and I feel that Mr. Cayce was here to show us a glimpse of that.

Let's have a look at what can we learn from your life, Mr. Cayce, from making possible what would seem to be impossible. Opening our eyes, is what I'm feeling, and seeing something new. Seeing in a way that we haven't seen before. We've experienced loss and seeing past that as well. This is also the energy of death and rebirth and transformation.

Completion of cycles. In the time that he lived there were things that the collective needed to learn then too.

The illumination, transformation, the light, bringing in the light. It's around feeling. I got a draw to the heart chakra when I was reading Mr. Cayce. I feel that the work he did, through the third eye, could not have been possible without activating the heart as well. I feel that the heart was critical, and that when we attempt to contact our higher selves, I don't think it's done through the third eye. It's through the heart. Often, it's done with the help of those around us. We underestimate how helpful we are to one another. That is a light-filled topic to talk about, he said, the way that we help one another. If we think back to the collective, that light, and the breaking away, and that vibrational frequency. We heal through helping one another.

The earth can provide us with much that can help to heal, because we are part of the earth's consciousness, because just like any other living being that inhabits this earth, we are part of the earth. There are things that we can discover that we haven't discovered yet around what she [Earth] can provide to heal us and help us. This is the same with our relationships with others. We haven't even touched the surface of how we can help, or how we do help one another. We may not know it because we are doing it at a collective consciousness level and a subconscious level. We don't understand the way that we help each other. If we did, there'd be less war and there'd be less fighting, and there'd be less factionalism.

Sometimes we feel that we must decide in the dark when, really, there should be no actual conscious decisions. If you were living in the light, or in that stream of consciousness, you would simply let go and go with the flow. He's saying sometimes, even though we're not there yet, that's all part of enlightenment to come to humanity.

I'm getting a lot of water energy in this reading. I'm getting a big draw to water. The healing power of water. What qualities are in the water, natural water, which support life? I'm getting a real draw to the things that you find in ponds, that they're able to grow and be sustained by simply being in that water. That, again, is something else that the earth can provide for us.

I'm getting control but I'm also getting gateway and the ability to steer that ship. That comes, I think, through co-operation with others, and through meeting people at the heart level, but also at the collective consciousness level as well.

The power of emotions will enable you to move mountains. Again, coming back to this consciousness, there is no confidence or lack of confidence if you're in touch with your higher consciousness. That doesn't even enter it.

I'm getting a draw also to emotions and attitudes. Those people who may not be confident, may not be operating at a high enough consciousness, because it's a moot point when you're at that level. For someone who is lacking self-worth or questioning their value, simply get in touch with your higher self, get in touch with your higher consciousness, and understand that that's where the real light of your being dwells.

I'm getting a pull also to current conditions, the world now. I understand that one of Mr. Cayce's predictions was around Russia being a peacemaker. It's anything but at the moment, but I feel in time, this prophecy will be seen to be true.

Again, changing the vibration, whatever the events are, as we move through the decades or the years to come, whatever those events are, however the current situations end, will result in parts of the world that are not on the same vibrational frequency now, joining that frequency. We don't know how Russia is going to lead us in the next decade. We only can see what we're seeing right now. I'm feeling that there is an evolution taking place. It's constant and it's growing.

Going back to the past. He's telling me or he's giving me the idea that if you want to know your future, go back to the past. He's saying that we know that we all have the keys to open those doors, and that we inherently know or intuitively know what needs to be done.

I am getting the importance of coming back to the collective, coming back to the self, coming back to the light. We are only young now and we've got a lot of climbing to do, and most of the time we do it the hard way. We don't understand that we can go more quickly. We are still on the treadmill. We are still focused entirely on this earth plane. We are not living at that higher consciousness level.

I'm probably going to finish with the cards here because the Six of Swords in the tarot deck is movement. This boat in the water moving away from troubled times. The energy of this card is both a Mercury and Aquarius. That's important. This card is important, something around that planetary configuration, because Mr. Cayce understood and used astrology to give him an initial idea of things. That somehow is important. That configuration is important to this reading. I feel that we will move into calmer waters in time, but first we need to understand why we have this disparity in this energetic vibration. Why we've got such divergence of energetic vibration at this time, and that there is a healing of the collective that needs to take place for us to move out of those troubled waters.

Let me just check and see if there's anything else that Mr. Cayce wants to bring through. I think he's saying no, and I'm just seeing the light.

I hope you enjoyed that almost impromptu channeling. I went with the flow. Hopefully, there are things in there that resonate with you. Thank you again.

Channeling Robin Williams
(Mental Health)

The late actor and comedian Robin Williams was universally admired for his humanity, wit and intellect. When he passed, the world mourned. I connected with his energetic vibration in October 2019. This was a particularly poignant channeling because he had taken his life a few years earlier and, as an empath, I had seen that darkness in someone close before. I still remember an image given to me from that session, a young Robin Williams running up his driveway/road home. He ran so fast, and the joy on his face was indescribable. I like to think he is doing that in the afterlife.

I'd like to do a channeling this morning of Robin Williams. Some of you, or most of you, would know Robin Williams. He's been around me for a while, on and off. He's been coming in and out. He first presented with a message around spontaneity and generating an energy when you're feeling unmotivated, some of the ways that you can generate energy when you don't feel energetic.

The various messages he's been bringing forward this morning are around energy and the brilliance of thought. Some people can connect very quickly with energy and their thoughts mirror this. I got the image this morning of a young boy running. Now, I don't know where Robin Williams was brought up, or even if this image is relating to him, but there is a road and there is a young boy running. There's also somebody on a veranda calling him. I'm not sure what that image means but he has been pacing. I don't know if it's restlessness.

Yes, he's telling me it is restless energy and the ability to get a "run-on" thought. If you've seen some readers, for example, they might not stop talking — more a channeling, it's that kind of thing. It's like when he joins in the thoughts, I guess inspired thoughts, and then he can access a continual stream. It's a bit like that young boy running. It just goes very, very quickly.

This morning I've got someone mowing my lawns in the background, and I wasn't going to do this session, but I was guided to keep going with it because what Robin Williams is trying to tell me is that in the latter part of his life [there was pain]. There's this youthful energy and the brilliant career that he had, based on his brilliant capacity to use his mind, but I'm also getting that there was pain, obviously at the end of his life.

He's saying to me that this hum, this noise that I've got now distracting me, which continually stops the run-on [of thoughts], was what he felt at the end of his life. That is what he didn't want to live with. Somebody that had lived freely and forcefully. When he experienced this run-on of thoughts as I describe it, he didn't necessarily even know where he was going, he just ran.

He had this ability to gather thoughts together. At the starting point would be two or three thoughts that would resonate. He would just go with it. It would be like a journey and a destination so that by the time he got to the end of that, he had taken people with him. It was the speed; it was the alacrity. It was like witnessing an Olympic runner in action because I'm continually getting this vision or this image of this young boy running, running, running.

He channeled that energy because it is — it's not quite ADHD, attention deficit syndrome. It's not quite that, but there are elements of mental health management that Robin Williams also had to contend with. He had to find an outlet for this energy, this quick energy, this restless energy. Even now as I see him, he's pacing. He's pacing. He's got his arms folded, and he's pacing. He told me before, if I go ahead with this reading this morning, I would not be sorry, even though I've got the lawnmower in the background. He's saying it's not going to distract me, but he wanted to illustrate what it was like for him at the end of his life where he just couldn't continue to do the things that he did, and he was in some pain because of that.

He also knew that it was only going to get worse. It's a bit like dignity in dying. He had a terminal illness that was going to really... he would have ended up in a vegetative state, almost. I don't like to use that terminology, but he would've ended up without any capacity at all, let's just put it like that, and reliant on other people. He didn't want to do that. While the world was rocked by his self-harm and the way that he passed, it was absolutely the right thing for him to do.

He's asking me to ask you to think about it in the same way that we have euthanasia, in the same way that we have dignity in dying. He's asking you to think about it in that regard. He's saying that he thought about it over a long period of time. He knew his prognosis. He didn't let on with other people, the people that he loved because he didn't want to draw them into it or upset them, or that they might stop him.

He understood that this was the only thing he could do, really, to keep his dignity and take matters into his own hands, take control of the situation because the illness for somebody who had had that sheer brilliant, mental alacrity, for someone to get dementia was such a random out of the blue happening, it was like a hammer blow. It was the last thing that he expected. There are lessons in there for him. There are lessons in allowing and taking enjoyment in thoughts being out of control, almost verging on manic. Absolutely there is.

There's also a freedom in thoughts being out of control. When I say out of control, if you think about the Chariot in the tarot, it's like you hang on for the ride because it's going to be fun but there's also a lesson in there as well and the lesson is around discipline. He was always well intentioned with his humor, always well intentioned.

I asked him what tarot deck I should be using this morning, and I thought about using my 78 Tarot Mythical deck.

I was very drawn to the artistry in that deck, but I got the impression that I was to use the Crow Tarot. He says that some people don't like the Crow Tarot because it can be quite confronting, particularly that Death card depicting a crow picking over the carcass but he's saying that the humor that he used was designed to make people think of things in another way, to confront them.

In doing so, in making them laugh about that, it was making people think of things in another way, in a different way, so that it's taking away their fear. The dementia that he was diagnosed with, Lewy body, is severe. That did scare him because of that lack of control. As I said, there's some kind of lesson there in discipline for him in going on the "Chariot ride" without holding onto the reins.

He had a hell of a ride in his life, but did he always go in the right direction, because he didn't really know where he was heading in terms of when he was in that stream, did he always go in the right direction? He's saying just a "little" more control would've been good.

Why is he coming through here today? He's got a big message around spontaneity. He's talking about when you're in that depressed state, which he was at the end of his time here in this incarnation. He's talking about when you're lying on the couch, when you can't get motivated, when the energy is just so heavy that you stop that run. He's talking about spontaneity as a way of raising the energy. It's allowing a glimmer of spontaneity to come into your thoughts.

He's saying look up. Instead of looking down, look up, look at something around you. There is inspiration in everything, he's saying, everything. That's why he could talk in the way that he could. He would look at something and it would just start that thought process, and off he would run. It could be as simple as a clock on the wall, tick tock, tick tock. It could be a picture, a family scene. I'm just looking around the room now and I'm being drawn to the outside. For me, my inspiration is outside in nature. What would get me up off the couch, if I was in that state, would be my love of the outdoors. My love of nature. He's saying, look up and start to observe and notice things around you. That is a way of stimulating your motivation.

It's human not to be motivated; it's human to be a little bit down at times. That's life. That's what we contend with here on this earth. If you can find some way of inspiring yourself through spontaneity, it could just change the shift for you. It can shift the focus for you. It can just generate that little bit of energy that will push you forward in some way.

There are messages around allowing your thoughts to go right out as far as they can go. There's always a need to stay grounded and be anchored. On the positive side, there's also a message here around free-flowing speech. When I opened up for this reading with the lawnmower in the background, I noticed how tight my throat was (this also ties in with the way Mr. Williams passed). The throat chakra is, of course, the chakra that aligns with communication and the color blue. When I look at blue, I'm looking right out now at the blue sky. The blue sky is endless.

When I noticed that my throat chakra was constricted, and so part of this running speech that Robin Williams had or has because he's still got it where he is now, is that he didn't have any constriction or restriction. There are two sides of a coin in everything. In a way, his ability to really talk at the speed of light was both a blessing and a curse. Before the dementia diagnosis there were periods where he was manic, and he's acknowledging that. I am getting the image of the Chariot card there.

Great, the ride was fantastic and a brilliant one, but there was always a need for discipline. If you're going to go out there to the edge, just make sure that you're anchored in some way. That goes for every feeling, emotion, situation, event where you are going beyond yourself. Always be anchored and be grounded. There are ways of doing that.

He's saying that sometimes we don't even realize that we're not grounded, and it's not until we start to feel unwell, or we start to feel a little bit uncomfortable, or we start to want to go home, he's saying, because there's this idea about getting up off the couch. When we're feeling this way, it can often be that we just need to ground ourselves, bring ourselves back a bit, have that little bit of discipline. We can start this process by starting to notice the things around us.

There is a mental health aspect in why he's come through here today. I haven't researched Robin Williams before this channeling. I know him from his career on the TV and I know his battle with dementia, and I know about his, very, very sad passing. He doesn't want people to be sad. He wants to reframe it. That's another reason that he's here. He wants to reframe it for us to look upon it as dignity in dying. Rather than looking upon it as self-harm, he's asking us to look upon it in the same way we would if someone euthanized themselves with stage four terminal cancer. He knew the end. He knew what the end would be like. He had spoken about his diagnosis. He knew exactly the path of the incurable disease. He knew that and he didn't want that for himself.

He's saying the biggest regret he had was he kept that so silent from everybody, from those around him, from his loved ones. It was an awful shock not just for his loved ones, but for the world and for his fans. He couldn't see that at the time, he was so depressed, so clinically depressed that he couldn't really see any other way out.

Let me ask Robin Williams to bring through the messages, the most important messages that he thinks we need to hear. What is it that he wants to tell us?

Glorious sunny day here in Australia. Blue skies. The kind of day where you would like to get outside, be inspired. Get up off the couch. All right, so, what does he want us to know? What does he want us to hear? He's saying that we are all wonderful. He said he could go on and on and on, how long is a piece of string, about how wonderful we are.

What messages does he want to bring through my Crow Tarot with the crows eating the carcass in the Death card? He thinks that's hilarious. Okay, so the first card out is the Moon and he's talking about the reflection. Reflections of ourselves can often be found in the situations that we try and hide.

It's important to allow things to come to the surface so that we don't bury them down 300 miles of ocean, so that they're never going to surface. It's important for us to chip away and keep chipping away. It doesn't matter how old we get. Keep chipping away at the things that we know we need to air, and we know we need to clear because ultimately, if we don't, they will lead, in one way or another, to a crisis of faith. He's talking about suffering here and how to alleviate suffering.

We've got the Wheel of Fortune. This is always knowing that you're going to have times where it's going to be fantastic and you're going to have times when it's challenging, but always knowing that things do pass and that things do move on. It is how you deal with the weaknesses, how you deal with the lows that really forges, in a very meaningful way, your strength and endurance.

He's also reminding me again that his mind was going, and he couldn't be strong. The strongest thing he could do while he still had his mind was to do what he did.

The Magician. This is actualizing [dreams, hopes, plans] into reality. Knowing that all troubles do pass. Why do they pass? They pass because we want them to pass.

The Devil card is probably one of the most mystifying cards to me in the tarot. It often comes forward as being unknowable. The traditional meaning is greed. It can come forward to indicate addictions. It can indicate substance addictions, love addictions, things that aren't for our highest good. It can even indicate this constant need to analyze. What is it? Paralysis by analysis can even be represented by this card. It can also be the great awakener. It can also be a sharp slap of a lesson.

It's underneath the Moon card and that, to me, is telling me that the more that we bring things to the surface, the more we air them, the more we understand our strengths and our weaknesses and bring our weaknesses to the surface, and our strengths as well.

He is telling me not to get into the Pollyanna type of Sunday school [sentiment], because that was another image that I got, someone hitting a triangle. I'm not sure if he went to Sunday school when he was young, but he said don't fall into those patterns either. You can bring your strengths to the surface just as much as you can bring your weaknesses. It's your choice. It's your choice, but you can't really bring your strengths to the surface if you don't understand what your weaknesses are. It's a concurrent process, and people often forget that.

They'll either do one or the other. If we understood how concurrent it is, we would have more control. This is sometimes why the Devil card appears in a spread. It's to understand strength and weakness concurrently: strength, weakness, power, disempowerment. I'm getting a very strong message there. Thank you, Spirit.

Having to defend oneself — that's clarifying the Wheel of Fortune. There's an upward energy. That's what I'm feeling with this card; there's an upward energy in defending oneself. It's, again, not just looking at the negative, but looking at the positiveness in standing your ground. This is another reason why I got the phrase *dignity in dying*. There is this upward energy that he wants to create around the circumstances of his passing, and to ask us to think of it in another way. I feel that's very important to him.

Clarifying the Magician is the Two of Pentacles. The number two is collaborating with others, networking. This is the juggling here, and this is making decisions. He is saying, when you're depressed, and there is a strong mental health overlay in this reading, when you're in that "lying on the couch" situation, another way to move forward is to rejoin your community.

I'm just going to keep going for another three cards here. The Knight of Cups. This is this energy, this quick, quick energy and it is very, very seductive. It's very, very alluring to be seduced by your weaknesses, but I'm understanding that the strengths and weaknesses, again, are two sides of the same coin.

The Knight of Cups traditionally represents an offer of love. He's allowing me to feel the strength and the positivity of love. You can allow that to come forward in spades. He's telling me, allow it to come forward in spades. Yes, it's an upward flow.

The Empress in the tarot represents abundance. Sometimes I see this card as having connections to the afterlife. For him, this upturn in energy, things changing … he found that after he passed. He found a movement onwards in the afterlife. This is again why he's telling me that what he did was absolutely the right thing to do. That's the strong message in this reading from him.

I've had my battle with illness, and I have been at the bedside with my relatives as well. I understand why some people support the concept of euthanasia. That instead of having four weeks or two months of suffering, whatever the timeline is, euthanasia can be merciful. There's stigma that we must overturn in relation to euthanasia, and the process of dying with dignity.

We have states in Australia which have approved euthanasia with all the right caveats. Checks and balances. It's not for everybody. For those that have a religious point of view to bring forward here, it is respected and acknowledged but for him, there's a message here that he wants to get through.

The Ace of Cups is also clarifying the Magician card, and I'm going to the Knight of Cups as well. Strong emotions. Thoughts will often trigger strong emotions. If you keep your thoughts strong, if you acknowledge your strengths, your weaknesses, if you love not hate, it's as simple as that, then you can generate the right kind of emotional environment for yourself.

At the base of this reading is the Four of Wands, which, of course, is celebrations, reunions with oneself and reunions with his family too. I feel that he has spent a lot of time looking after his family, parenting his children, being around for those that he loved because these were the people he hurt the most with his silence, and with the way that he chose to leave this world.

He's saying, when you look around, when you get up off that couch, when you start to be inspired, miracles can happen.

He's saying, look for those, because it really is life-affirming. He saw a lot of miracles. He's just saying, believe in miracles. Then they can be found even in the darkest of places.

I'm going to leave that there. As I said, I was going to put this off because of that mowing but I felt it was there for a reason. One of the things that he wanted to get across was not to be too hard on him for what he did. He said that is a message that goes for all people that unsubscribe from life. He is saying that they do what they do at that time for a reason. He's saying not to forget the reason, not to let the way that things happen to overshadow the reason.

I'm going to leave it there. I don't know if you enjoyed that channeling, but I hope that it has resonance for you in some way. I'm just going to close now. [silence] I'm getting the thumbs up here. We're done. We're finished.

I'm getting the … I don't know whether it's a crow or it's a dove. It doesn't really matter. I'm getting the bird ascending now. All right, I'll leave that there. Thank you.

Spiritual Aspects of Health …
A Higher View

I have a playlist called the Spirit Files on my YouTube channel devoted to channelings on various themes. In June 2022, after a particularly difficult year dealing with COVID, food sensitivities, and allergies, I was called to channel health messages. As with all my channelings, it feels like I am having a direct conversation with Spirit.

Today I wanted to ask if there is a spiritual aspect to health. Indeed, I know that to be true. As many of you know, in 2014/15, I was diagnosed with cancer. I went through years of treatment which involved chemotherapy and radiation, two surgeries and then a long rehabilitation and recovery process.

Before cancer, I had been diagnosed with autoimmune diseases, allergies, and sensitivities.

I'd always been sensitive, but the older I got, the more the body wore down. Back then, I had no real idea how to manage my health issues and, I largely ignored them. It culminated in a health crisis that changed my life — a complete 360. So, when I ask if there is a spiritual aspect of health, I am asking about the growth of the soul, and the soul's growth is reflected in the way that we evolve. Learning is not just 3D, is it? It's all encompassing.

We come into the world, and we go through various processes and at the end of our lives, hopefully, knowing, with gratitude and love and wisdom, that there are higher sources and much more than we see in our 3D living. So, I equate my health journey with a spiritual journey. It's never easy and we can fall back into the traps and patterns that caused the health problems. You know that it's not good for you and you try and stay strong. Like all life learning, you wade through the patterning and habitual behaviors to realize the truth. And often you regress and then you progress and fall back yet again.

That's the way it's gone for me.

I have multiple planets in Sagittarius, and Venus in Scorpio in the Sixth House. My Mars in Sagittarius is just slightly into the Seventh House. The Sixth House, for those of you that don't know, is the House ruled by Virgo and is the House of work, public service, sacrifice, everyday routines, and the House of health/illness. If I had looked at my chart early in life, if I was an astrologer back then, for example, I would've said, "Okay, what am I going to do to really, really understand this and do the right thing by my health?" But you don't have that sort of wisdom as a teenager or young adult. Wisdom arrives with time.

The aspects in my natal chart, the good and the bad, all painted a bigger picture. Looking back on it, and just recently having had another health crisis, which didn't involve cancer, but did involve allergies, sensitivities, autoimmune issues, I have to say, yet again, Spirit was trying to tell me something. In fact, I had a very powerful dream amid feeling unwell.

I'm very mindful, [post-cancer] that I must pace myself now.

I had this dream during the pinnacle of my 2022 year of ill health. I dreamed I was chasing myself with a knife and was continually stabbing myself in the gut, a horrible dream. I somehow knew that this person, "me," had been chasing "me" all my life. Eventually, "me" caught up to "me" with the knife. In the dream state I surrendered to the chase I'd been running from all my life. "Do your best," and this person, the other "me" said: "Well, I'll just do it to myself." This person, the other "me," then stabbed and killed themselves. I don't know what [psychiatrists] Jung and Freud would've made of that dream.

I suspect I know.

It was an unpleasant dream, and when I awoke it was with the thought that I'm somehow doing this to myself.

All year I'd been consulting with multiple doctors who couldn't figure out what was wrong with me. I'm angry with them because they should have been able to diagnose through research, trial, and elimination.

However, through the dream and with intuition, I knew what was wrong, and I changed what needed to be changed in my diet. Miraculously, the allergies and sensitivities were identified. I solved the problem when they couldn't.

What does that say? I guess if I wasn't tuned into my dreams, if I hadn't been thinking about this, if I hadn't been proactively and assertively confronting and trying to solve my health issues, including from a spiritual dimension, I would still be struggling in the dark. I would be sick and likely getting worse.

We compartmentalize ourselves but when we take that holistic, wider view, which includes a spiritual view, we can be led to solutions.

So, is there a spiritual dimension to our health? The first card I am getting is the Shaman card and from that I am getting completion. So really that's a strong answer from Spirit because the shaman is a holistic wisdom gatherer and healer.

The shaman listens to nature, but it's not just about nature being external from us; it is about internal processes, and connection.

Negativity in all its guises has an impact and you generally know it when it's influencing you. However, sometimes, it's difficult to see the "woods from the trees" when you're dealing with any sort of crisis. Often, I lag in action, and I shouldn't; I should act straight away as soon as I feel an energy impact. There are always solutions. Why do we not do enough? Why don't we step back? Instead, we're always busting on into that fray, rather than rising above it. There's the idea that we've got to fill our days with trivia, the unimportant, and often [redundant] action. I think healing happens when you stop and do what you need to do to gather that wisdom, even if it's taking the time to do a deep and intuitive dive.

The getting of wisdom doesn't occur when you bury your head in the sand, nor does it come about by pushing forward without hindsight. Sometimes we just need to find a middle ground and nurture ourselves. Nothing grows without care. I have a very rare plant that only grows in tropical areas. It's such a beautiful plant. I've been nurturing it and it's growing even though I don't live in a tropical climate. Nothing thrives without nurture, including ourselves and our health.

Sometimes we've also got to get innovative and motivated about our health.

Our journeys are ongoing. Growing is not static, and that's how we move forward in a cycle of birth and renewal. So, dream; dream your solutions. Throw it out there before you go to sleep and ask with intention: what is the solution to this?

Sustenance – I want to make a point of saying, because often readings can be so heavy, you need to include self-expression. In fact, whenever you lose yourself, talk, speak. I don't care if you say "the sun's purple today," even if you say something random. Sing through your tight throat. Express yourself.

Back to our fundamental question: Does health have a spiritual aspect? Resilience is a key theme here. Even during the darkest storms, there is illumination within. Be your own guiding light. Never give up. We get to a point sometimes where we must surrender to the flow, but when we surrender, we don't just close ourselves off, we surrender to a calling of our inner voice and wisdom.

We stop and we allow that to come forward. This is about being determined, and determination doesn't include carrying on regardless, and not learning. It includes stopping and listening and setting an intention. Then when you've got the answer, moving on. That's the definition of not giving up.

Partnerships – the unconditional and the simplicity of loving connections. We always need other people around us. Even if we are living on our own, partnerships can include the people we meet as we go to the post office; those in our community; being with others is important. We're not an island; we are surrounded by our community.

Renaissance – Create your own masterpiece. This is about expression and creating in whatever way you create.

Communication – That's what I was looking for. We are more than we think. Observe your thoughts because they do precede your words.

Adversity – Honor your energy here. The ebb and flow of life lessons and afterwards the learning remains.

Meditation – Observe your thoughts. Let the negative flow away and feel your energetic vibration rise. Meditation allows us to connect to our inner self and our inner self is wise. So, if you've forgotten the lesson, I'm sure it will come back. It will come back intuitively to you, but you've got to stop and listen to yourself. Allow the thoughts to arise and let them flow away because insight, third eye insight, and spiritual insight, come from a place of stillness, and stillness is flow, not rigidity.

One of the key questions regarding our health is what do we need to notice? Health has a spiritual dimension. I think we've established it does. What do we need to know about our health and the way we can improve it through this holistic view? The theme of channeling comes through. So, you can channel thought from your guides. Those loved ones that have passed away. They're always around to give you strength. Even your inner guide, your inner knowing, your intuition, you can channel that. All these things can be helpful at a time when we're in our biggest need.

Transformation – I love that. You know, when I figure something out after a lesson that's particularly difficult, I feel it's all part of a transformation.

Remembrance – I think this is remembering who we are, remembering where we came from. They're big, big statements. Remembering where we came from and being comfortable with that. That's when we cut through almost everything, don't we? We cut through the noise. We remember where we came from.

You Are the Universe – and you contain everything within you. Everything. Everything. And finally, expansion. That's what we're always going for, aren't we?

The Soul's Expansion – Expansion that's where we are and where we're going. Whether we're Christian or Seventh Day Adventist or Catholic, it's all about expansion. Even if you are speaking about reincarnation and the soul's journey, at the end of everything and at the beginning of everything and in the middle of everything, it is all about the soul's expansion.

When We Ask "Why?" …
The Collective Is Creating a New Story

I had just been through months of ill health and, finally, I began to experience a return to strength, and a willingness to open my energy again up to the channel I had with Spirit. In July 2022, after the invasion of Ukraine by Russia and documented war crimes, along with the instability of the US, and the end of the COVID pandemic in sight, I felt it was time to ask that perennial question we always do when events, circumstances and relationships are destructive and shocking — the question: why?

The orbs have been showing up lately. My health has been getting stronger and stronger, and I'm more able to raise my vibration. And so, the orbs are back. Also, they're quite protective as well. Thank you to those that have commented generally on the videos. Thank you to those who have supported this channel.

I have a lot of gratitude for you for doing that. Today, there is a multitude of things that I could read on, but I really want to just do something for the collective. What is the information we need to know at this time? If you're like me, you're thinking, well, will things ever go back to normal? We have here, in Australia, a third wave of Covid. It's quite scary again with hospitalizations and ICU and death numbers rising.

We are all trying to stay in good health and manage as best we can in Australia now, with our third wave. We are in the middle of winter, and this is why we've been hit so hard with it. In my predictions, I did say Covid was not gone. And although we wanted it to be gone, it wasn't, and I think that's what we're seeing now. Will it be gone in the future? Yes. Will this war mongering march toward authoritarianism be checked? Someone sent me a link to a podcast recently that talked about these sacrifices that our grandparents, my father, my grandparents, my uncles gave in the various world wars and the other wars, Vietnam, and Korea. They fought to stop this march of authoritarianism, just as Ukraine is doing. However, Putin, the war criminal, has tried in many ways to blackmail the West including cutting off gas supplies as Europe heads into winter, crippling the economies, and raising the inflation. He's now attempting to block food supplies to the developing world so that there's an influx of asylum seekers, starving refugees, across the borders. He's done this before, and so still we sit here, and we wait. In America, democracy is in crisis. So, taking all those things into consideration, I want to read today for the Collective. Will things get back to normal? What are the essential messages that we need to know as a Collective? Where are we heading? Why is this happening?

The first card embodies the theme of the oracle card *Codes of the Seeds*. The blueprint is within you; take the next step. The blueprint, the codes of the seeds, meaning what are we growing and, more importantly, what have we planted? We all have a blueprint and, collectively, we have a blueprint too. Our purpose is what makes us move through a timeline. What makes us choose a particular timeline? It is our blueprint which is destined from birth.

The second card is the *Return, a New Story*. You decide on what it is that you're aligned to, and we come together somewhere in all this madness, in all this insanity, in all this tragedy and there is a new story. Now, if you look at your intuition, and I mean really look at it, you can move away from conspiracy theories; from your fundamentalism, from being judgmental and intolerant. Move away from that noise and use your intuition instead. Use that force within you and your intuition should tell you that we are creating a new story.

The Great Mother – Surrender to the mystery, fall into her arms. When you do that, you will feel relief from your burdens.

Mother Earth. We are part of Mother Earth, we're part of nature, and nature has her own story, and journey.

The High Priestess – the unknown. What comes to the surface? Often in the tarot, the High Priestess is holding a book that is yet to be written or perhaps is written but not told. A new story. The energy that is propelling us in this journey is hidden in plain sight within the mysteries, learning and teaching.

The more we surrender to the new story that is being created, the more we look for what is hidden, and we learn and then we teach. That is infinite wisdom that nobody can argue with because it is not within their reach if they haven't surrendered to that new story.

Trust the Seasons – embracing change, the cycles of life; transition and change. Trust that we are creating a new story. Trust in our ability to create a new story. Trust in the past, trust in the present, and trust in the future.

What is this new story that we are creating? What we need to know is hidden in plain sight. I'm hearing that it is in our DNA, and it's also around survival. We don't just survive, do we? We always look to thrive. What is this new story that we are creating? It is movement forward. It is progress. What is hidden in plain sight is progress. I know some of you are going to say, *you lost me there because we are regressing*. However, think about how bizarre the regressions are now. It's like a psychosis. What do we do when we're confronted with crisis? Think of a health crisis that you've had and one where you are looking at your own mortality.

You would be anxious, experiencing high anxiety levels about the future. We want to grasp hold of what was, what we think was better in the past, and this can create ill health. There is one thing that is inevitable and that is change. Well, I can think of another that's inevitable, and that is the truth, however uncomfortable.

Emerging – Change and the truth are hidden in plain sight. We are being offered something. At this time in our existence, we might feel that there's constant surprises, constant challenges, constant, constant, constant. However, we are being challenged by change, to change.

Not only is our intuition growing stronger, but our logic is activated because chaotic events and crises are challenging our survival. What do we need to do? Each of you will have your own answers to that. The way that I embrace that is to create the best environment that I can to stay as healthy as I can. To connect spiritually, to embrace faith and grace. That's surrendering, and logical as well. Each of us has that ability within us. We need not wait until the end; we can do that now.

We have both the subconscious intuitive side, and we also have the logical, conscious side. We're not without power in these situations.

If you translate that to the Collective, you'll see that we are more powerful than we think. We are manifesting the first step we are taking in this new story that we are creating. We have already realized this in the past and yet, we set these events in motion at some level. We took that step. Even if the step was awareness that our earth was in peril, *is in peril*. Through transforming, through transmigration, through a process of moving through change, there is the potential for great victories. We will manifest what we need.

Remember Europe did not give in to the Russian President Vladimir Putin's blackmail and threats; instead, it united against him in a very powerful way that history will enshrine. We are more powerful than we think. When we give into our fears, we surrender that logical analytical part of our mind, and we move into conspiracy theories and fear itself.

Logic is a series of steps that can propel us to the future. It's the tool that we should be using. It is important for everybody to nurture, nurture themselves, nurture loved ones, nurture the earth, nurture your immediate environment, experience and feel love. It's a good antidote. It really is a good antidote to these troubled times.

The external environment can be deceptive. There are those that seek to steal. What are they stealing? In some cases, they are stealing democracy, freedoms and liberty.

However, the revelations that are emerging and the sacrifice in the past, present and future to establish truth will ensure that democracy does not fail. It does not crumble. And that sacrifice is demanded of all of us in whatever way we can contribute because we are part of the Collective.

Let's just look at our fear. Our fear is that we're at the crossroads; we know it, and we may make the wrong decision. The march of authoritarianism, the loss of freedom, the regression to the past, this mass psychosis. What are we choosing? Can we choose correctly? Logic and wisdom will prevail, not fear and conspiracy. Psychosis is temporary albeit acute.

I've said over the years that one of the things that will save us is the rising of the Divine Feminine. That is not said to isolate the Divine Masculine. There must be a balance. So, all that nurtures, all that loves, knows that to have a future, life must be sustained. The Queens in the tarot bring forward stability. Stability through law, stability through planning, stability through strategy, through resilience and sustainability, and through self-care and love. The Queens use everything at their disposal to establish stability. *Logic,* we are heading away from mass psychosis towards planning for our future, towards strategy, and law not chaos.

Why did we need to do this? Confusion. We were confused. I guess most of were confused about this idea that we are separate from one another. The creed of the MAGA movement in the US, is separation. "We don't want to be joined with you anymore, but we also want power over you too. We don't just want to do our thing and let you do your thing. No, we want power over you too." There's a separation here. However, I believe still in miracles. The underlying energy is in miracles, and our emotional needs being realized.

This is the destination.

We do have to be patient and we do have to plan for what we want to manifest, and we need to retain control of that manifestation. We do have to bring this all together in this process, along this journey to, ultimately, regain stability and forward momentum. This is the process toward our new story. Our new story is not separation, it is unity.

Let's have a look at where this timeline goes? This current timeline, the blueprint timeline, the new story. Let's have a look at where that goes?

Some will be lost. Lessons need to be learned. Choices need to be made. This is the reality. This is the reality that we live in. We do need to support one another. When we do this, we successfully move through these times, moving out as I often say, of troubled waters. So right now, we have deception and theft and the need to learn and teach the lessons. We do have serious, serious choices to make.

And you're seeing them being made in Europe and you're seeing them being made in America right now — from the doctor who performed the abortion on the 10-year-old rape victim in a state where abortion had been banned, and the state's attorney general is now trying to sue her. The doctor made the choice. What other choice could she make? The Attorney General has also made a choice, as have Republicans in America who are attempting to overturn elections. Putin murdering Ukrainian children, has made a choice (in Israel and Gaza, choices were also made to slaughter innocent children). What choice are we going to make? Are we going to stand against this as our fathers, our grandfathers, our cousins, our uncles, have — the brave people that have stood up to be counted? What choices are we going to make?

The mystery of humanity is around us in the sacrifices that we are prepared to make for others to create this new story. So, I think we all know that it's a tipping point right now, but we also know that we've got to stand shoulder to shoulder, not give up, and make the sacrifices. We know we need to create the freedom for our children, and for our grandchildren, in the same way that freedom was created for us. It's going to be okay, is what Spirit wants us to know. It's going to be okay. We'll come through this.

I'm going to post the introduction to this reading because I want you to see the orbs. There's been a few while I've been reading. Spirit is around and Spirit is helping me deliver this message to you.

Afterword – The Water Giver

Years ago, when I was traveling back and forth on my daily commute to Canberra, past the infamous and mysterious Lake George, I had what can only be described as an "out of body" experience. As I drove past the steep craigs and thick Australian bush, I "heard" or felt the sound of a deep beat. It wasn't perceived with my ears but rather my whole being. It was what I can only describe as the sound of the earth itself.

Lake George is an anomaly in Australia. It doesn't have a known water source and is an endorheic lake (a drainage basin that retains water and has no outflow). Water seems to appear during the rainy season and recede during the successive hot weeks and months. I've seen it almost bone dry, and full enough to lap the edges of the highway. This day was clear with blue skies and sun. It felt like I was driving into a haze with a pulsating, ever-present, earthly beat. I shook myself out of this state, as I was driving. A little unnerved, I continued on my way to work. I never forgot that day.

Around that time, I had a dream I will also never forget. I was at Lake George and alongside me walked an Aboriginal Elder. He showed me a landscape that was destroyed, but in the distance, beyond the blackened and broken trees, was the lake. He pointed at the lake and I understood I was to cross that barren ground by myself and that, one day, I'd reach the water. I became aware that there would be trials to undergo, but that reaching the water was the goal.

As with most things that come from these rich esoteric realms, it takes time, and experience, to understand their meaning. After that dream and my experience at Lake George, I lost my dad, my mum and my sister, and I went through cancer surgery, chemotherapy and radiation — all within years of one another. Life dealt me huge blows and the opportunity to grasp hope and have faith that the lessons would reveal to me a sanctuary of understanding and wisdom.

We've all been in this place, and we've all had to climb out of it, stronger than before.

I wrote about my dream at the time. I know that the place the Aboriginal Elder pointed to was a metaphor for coming back to my heart, changed yet renewed. In hindsight, the dream and the subsequent poem were prophetic.

Water giver
One day I remembered, what I was supposed to do.
I thought of the ground I had walked on,
This earth; this lifetime,
Across green fields, and dust, and fire,
Always towards the lake's edge. To the water.

I walked beside a guide on my journey.
I didn't look into his eyes; I feared that.
This Shaman.

I remember he pointed to the water,
A million miles away, across alien landscape,
Barren and destroyed by... I'm not sure.

I only knew I had to cross that wasteland,
With its dead trees and murky shadows,
To get to the water, for whatever his reason,
For pointing to it, as if I knew.

I remember now that water nourishes,
And quenches thirst.
It carries things away,

Like words and thoughts, and experiences,
And leaves something new, and clear.

I crossed that barren land ... like he said,
To find myself, and now to write these words.

O-BOOKS

SPIRITUALITY

O is a symbol of the world, of oneness and unity; this eye represents knowledge and insight. We publish titles on general spirituality and living a spiritual life. We aim to inform and help you on your own journey in this life.
If you have enjoyed this book, why not tell other readers by posting a review on your preferred book site?

Recent bestsellers from O-Books are:

Heart of Tantric Sex
Diana Richardson
Revealing Eastern secrets of deep love and intimacy to Western couples.
Paperback: 978-1-90381-637-0 ebook: 978-1-84694-637-0

Crystal Prescriptions
The A-Z guide to over 1,200 symptoms and their healing crystals
Judy Hall
The first in the popular series of eight books, this handy little guide is packed as tight as a pill bottle with crystal remedies for ailments.
Paperback: 978-1-90504-740-6 ebook: 978-1-84694-629-5

Shine On

David Ditchfield and J S Jones
What if the after effects of a near-death experience were
undeniable? What if a person could suddenly produce
high-quality paintings of the afterlife, or if they
acquired the ability to compose classical symphonies?
Meet: David Ditchfield.
Paperback: 978-1-78904-365-5 ebook: 978-1-78904-366-2

The Way of Reiki

The Inner Teachings of Mikao Usui
Frans Stiene
The roadmap for deepening your understanding
of the system of Reiki and rediscovering
your True Self.
Paperback: 978-1-78535-665-0 ebook: 978-1-78535-744-2

You Are Not Your Thoughts

Frances Trussell
The journey to a mindful way of being, for those who want
to truly know the power of mindfulness.
Paperback: 978-1-78535-816-6 ebook: 978-1-78535-817-3

The Mysteries of the Twelfth Astrological House

Fallen Angels
Carmen Turner-Schott, MSW, LISW
Everyone wants to know more about the most misunderstood
house in astrology — the twelfth astrological house.
Paperback: 978-1-78099-343-0 ebook: 978-1-78099-344-7

WhatsApps from Heaven
Louise Hamlin
An account of a bereavement and the extraordinary
signs — including WhatsApps — that a retired
law lecturer received from her deceased husband.
Paperback: 978-1-78904-947-3 ebook: 978-1-78904-948-0

The Holistic Guide to Your Health
& Wellbeing Today
Oliver Rolfe
A holistic guide to improving your complete health,
both inside and out.
Paperback: 978-1-78535-392-5 ebook: 978-1-78535-393-2

Cool Sex
Diana Richardson and Wendy Doeleman
For deeply satisfying sex, the real secret is to reduce the heat,
to cool down. Discover the empowerment and fulfilment
of sex with loving mindfulness.
Paperback: 978-1-78904-351-8 ebook: 978-1-78904-352-5

Creating Real Happiness A to Z
Stephani Grace
Creating Real Happiness A to Z will help you understand
the truth that you are not your ego
(conditioned self).
Paperback: 978-1-78904-951-0 ebook: 978-1-78904-952-7

A Colourful Dose of Optimism
Jules Standish
It's time for us to look on the bright side, by boosting
our mood and lifting our spirit, both in
our interiors, as well as in our closet.
Paperback: 978-1-78904-927-5 ebook: 978-1-78904-928-2

Readers of ebooks can buy or view any of these bestsellers by
clicking on the live link in the title. Most titles are published
in paperback and as an ebook. Paperbacks are available in
traditional bookshops. Both print and ebook formats are
available online.

Find more titles and sign up to our readers' newsletter at
www.o-books.com

Follow O-Books on Facebook at **O-Books**

For video content, author interviews and more, please subscribe to our YouTube channel:

O-BOOKS Presents

Follow us on social media for book news, promotions and more:

Facebook: O-Books

Instagram: @o_books_mbs

X: @obooks

Tik Tok: @ObooksMBS

www.o-books.com